The High Calling

Edwell Nhira

ISBN – 13:978-0-9974627-0-8
ISBN – 10:0997462701

Cover design by Ed McConnell Design

DEDICATION

This book is dedicated to evangelists, missionaries, pastors, supporters, and intercessors endeavoring to fulfill the Great Commission. Evangelists gather souls for the kingdom of God. Missionaries go to uncharted places to establish the kingdom of God. Pastors guard the flock that God entrusts to them. Supporters and intercessors make things happen by providing resources and prayer power.

This book is also dedicated to my family for their trust and relentless support on the journey to fulfill the Great Commission.

CONTENTS

FOREWORD

I have known Edwell Nhira for more than two decades. My first experience with him was as his academic advisor during his time as an undergraduate student at Oral Roberts University. Shortly after getting to know him and his wife, Constance, we invited them over to our home for dinner. That evening with Edwell, Constance, and their two children blossomed into a friendship that I am more than happy to say has continued and grown over the years.

I can tell you many things about Edwell. He was a good student. He earned many different university degrees. He is an excellent father. First and foremost, though, he is a man of God. I have been able to watch him from a distance as he has touched thousands of people—not only in the United States but around the world—with the Gospel. When I have been asked to introduce Edwell at different venues, I have always said, "It is my privilege to introduce to you one of the hardest working ministers and evangelists that I have ever had to work with: my friend, Dr. Edwell Nhira."

In this book, Edwell walks you through his and his family's spiritual journey. It is a journey that has been filled with challenges and victories. This book details the high calling the Lord placed on Edwell's heart. As you travel down this road of remembrance with him, you will see the hand of Jesus every step of the way. Each chapter screams: "Trust God!" This is a book that you not only will want in your library, but you will want to read it and then share it with your friends.

I was honored when Edwell asked me to write this foreword to this book, *The High Calling.* So now, I want to introduce you to my friend, and author, Dr. Edwell Nhira, the hardest working minister and evangelist I know.

Dr. James C. Tollett
Associate Professor at Oral Roberts University
Founder and President of James Tollett Ministries
Tulsa, Oklahoma

ACKNOWLEDGMENTS

My acknowledgements go to my parents, Edmond and Violet Nhira, who brought me into this world and who nurtured me until I was able to take care of myself. They got me started on my educational and life journey. I thank God for Christ who saved me, and for all the churches and leaders who helped mold me to be the man that I am today. I give my appreciation to the schools that I attended in all my years until now: Rukario Primary School, Murewa High School, Africa-Multination for Christ Institute, Christ for the Nations Institute, Oral Roberts University, University of Phoenix, Liberty University, and Northcentral University. I also appreciate the friends and family who have been sources of encouragement on this journey. I thank the board of our ministry, Hope for All Nations Ministries International, who persistently urged me to write this book. I especially thank those who have been very close and who have been bearing the burden of the journey with me: my wife, Constance, and our children Prosper, Jasper, Brian, Faith, my son-in-law, Gary II, and my grandchildren Nhira Lu and Tre.

INTRODUCTION

The High Calling is the result of friends and family demanding the writing of this autobiography. It is indeed an exciting recollection of the journey that I have walked these several decades. The journey began in a small Mbizi Village in Uzumba in Murewa, Zimbabwe. I was born at a small facility called Nyadire Hospital. I grew up in the village, and I attended nearby Rukariro School. I then went for secondary education at Murewa High School in 1972, a United Methodist Mission school. After finishing high school, I taught school at Guyu in Maramba, then moved to Kaseke in Uzumba. I moved to Rota School in Mangwende, then to Chinhenga School in Mukarakate. Due to the war for independence in Zimbabwe, schools in the rural areas shut down in 1978. Like many young people, I moved to the big city of Harare, where I stayed with my cousin Bernard Nhira and his family for seven months in Mufakose suburb. I gave my life to Christ while visiting my sister, who was staying with our Aunt Christine Chikore in Kambuzuma suburb. My Uncle Sherman Chikore helped me find a job at Textbook Sales Book Center in the accounts department.

In 1980, I got a job with Standard Chartered Bank. It was while I was working at the bank that the Lord called me into the ministry, just before I married my lovely wife Constance, whom I had met at Kambuzuma Ezekiel Chapel. Ten days after we got married, we packed our few belongings and went to Bible school at Africa Multination for Christ Institute in Glen Norah, Harare. After two years at the school, we were assigned to a Zimbabwe Assemblies of God Church in Tafara, where we pastored for two years. We were transferred to Waterfalls, where we pastored for a year, then we were moved to Mucheke Masvingo. We were sent to troubleshoot struggling churches, and when the problems were fixed, we were moved to another place. We pastored the Mucheke church for two years before the Lord opened a door for me to pursue my quest for education at Christ for the Nations Institute in Dallas, Texas, in 1989. Constance stayed pastoring the Mucheke church for a year while I was at CFNI. She followed after I had enrolled at Oral Roberts University in Tulsa, Oklahoma, in 1990 with our two children then, Jasper and Prosper. While in Tulsa, we had two more children: Brian and Faith.

At Oral Roberts University, I earned three degrees: a BA in Evangelism, an MA in Education, and an EdD in Educational Leadership. Then I completed an MBA in General Business at University of Phoenix at the Tulsa campus. I proceeded to pursue an MDiv and a DMin at Liberty University in Lynchburg, Virginia. I finally pursued a PhD in Global Training and Development at Northcentral University in Arizona.

In 1993, I took a ten-day mission trip to Montego Bay, Jamaica, during Spring Break. In 1994, I joined a summer mission team to Israel with Christ for the Nations Institute. In 1997, I started traveling on missions to different African countries with teams. After ministering in nine countries, the Lord instructed us to focus on Zimbabwe, my home country. Since 2003, each year we have taken teams of short-term missionaries, ranging from four to fifteen people. We have seen thousands of lives changed through the Word of God. We have started building a center for Evangelism and World Missions in Harare called Hope Center Zimbabwe.

CHAPTER 1
EARLY CHILDHOOD

I was born to Edmond and Violet Nhira in 1957 at Nyadire Hospital. For a while, my parents lived and taught at a school near Mbizi Village in rural Murewa District. Later my father trained to become a carpenter. In addition to being a carpenter, he was a subsistence farmer. In summer when the rains came, he would rise up early in the morning to go to plow the fields. Later in the day, he would come home to his carpentry shop. Mother stayed home and took care of me and my siblings, as well as helped in the fields. As I was growing up, she took me to the fields with other women of the village. When I became of age, I helped my father with the plowing, and later I helped in the carpentry shop. The Nhira clan took turns herding our cattle in the bushes. After school and on weekends, I herded the cattle when it was our family's turn.

Mbizi was one of the crowded remote villages in Murewa. There was no running water. There was no electricity. Water was fetched from a well about a mile away from our houses. At night, we used paraffin lamps or candles for light. For heating purposes, we used firewood, which was carried on our heads from several miles away from home. To relieve ourselves, we used pit latrines or the bush. We were content with that kind of life, and we did not know any other.

On Sundays, my parents took me to the village United Methodist Church which met at the nearby primary school. I enjoyed listening and following along as I could to the singing of hymns. It was really the faithful who went to church, because Sunday was a day to relax and go beer-drinking and partying for most village folk. My parents did not drink or smoke. We were taught to stay away from drinking and smoking. So we always looked forward to going to church on Sunday. The services were conducted by the lay leaders of the church. The church had a district minister who circulated around to about five or more of these churches. So he would come to our local congregation about once a month or once in two months. Although we did not have a born-again experience, I loved going to church and singing hymns.

As I was growing up, my duties at home were helping with the daily chores, like herding cattle, milking the cows with father, plowing the fields, and other things that needed to be done. During school time, I walked to school about five miles away from our home. The name of my primary school was Rukariro, which means “the hope.” I would make this trip daily with other kids from our village. My parents influenced me to like school. The village school was only primary level: from grade one to grade seven. Upon passing grade seven, one would go to secondary school somewhere else. I passed grade seven at the top of my class. I was accepted for secondary school at Murewa High School in 1972. Because there were very few high schools in the country, less than ten percent of the students from primary schools would proceed to some high school. So only two students from my primary school managed to go to secondary school.

CHAPTER 2
AT MUREWA MISSION

Murewa High School was a United Methodist Mission school about thirty miles away from our village. I really looked forward with great anticipation to moving away from home for the first time to go to boarding school. Murewa town was perhaps the largest town close to our village. It had a population of about 9000 people. It had a shopping center. Two bus companies had their hubs there. The nearest post office to the village where I grew up was there, as well as the district administration offices. The main hospital was situated there. So when one went to Murewa town from where we lived, one had gone to the big city, compared to the small stores that were close to us. Murewa High School was just two miles north of Murewa town. I really felt elated to move away from home to live in this big city.

It took all of my father's savings from his cotton field to send me to high school that first year. When I first arrived at Murewa, in January 1972, I felt apprehensive as this was my first time away from home. There were about 320 students at the school. Most of them lived at the school, even if their homes were close by. A new chapter in my life had begun.

Elisha Karimazondo and I were the only two students from Rukariro, our village primary school, who made it to high school, due to the bottleneck of many students who applied at the grade seven level throughout Zimbabwe schools for the few high school openings in the 1970s. We felt quite privileged to go to Murewa High. We quickly became friends, even though before we came to this school we knew each other but were not quite friends. At the school there were two streams of classes from Form 1 to Form 4. Elisha and I were in two different classes, but we would see each other often around school, which was comforting. One other comforting thing was that a cousin of mine, Godfrey Makawa, from a distant village from where we lived, also made it to Murewa High from Chitimbe Primary school the same year that I did.

The classes that we took included English, mathematics, science, Shona (our native language), geography, history, commerce, bookkeeping, typing, and building. I liked English, mathematics, and Shona the most. I made good grades most of the time. I was usually in the top ten of my class (the two streams combined with a total of about eighty students). We went to school Monday through Friday from seven in the morning to one o'clock. Lunch break was from one o'clock to two o'clock with a thirty-minute siesta. At two, we went back to school until four. After four, we went for extracurricular activities. Dinner was between five and six. Monday through Thursday, from seven to nine at night, we went back to school for studies. Friday night we had social functions in the school cafeteria hall. We would see a movie, play records, listen to prepared speeches, or hear debates. Our social functions master was Mr. James Murwira. He was the school's deputy headmaster and a disciplinarian.

The headmaster of our school, Mr. Alec Chibanguza, was also a no-nonsense man. He would be heard saying, "You have to behave here. You can fool around, but not after you come into the four walls of my office." One day one of my teachers was away. So, for his class, we were told to read and do some assignments in the classroom. Instead of doing the work that we were assigned, we began to talk and play around during that class time. The headmaster heard the noise that we were making and he hurried to our class. When he came in, he demanded that those who were talking stand up immediately. One by one the noise makers began to stand, as he sternly looked at the whole class. I was one of those who stood up. About six or seven of us stood up. We were rushed to his office, and we sure "got it." We were spanked as we were never spanked before in our lives. I will not forget that day.

We stayed busy most of the time for the four years while I was at Murewa High. Our time revolved around waking up early in the morning to prepare for the day, going for breakfast, going to school, going to lunch, going back to school, going to extracurricular activities, going for dinner, going back to school for night study and going back to the dormitory to sleep. Our school year was divided into three terms. The first term was from January to April. We would have a three-week break. The second term was from May to August, and we would have another three-week break. The third term was from September to early December, followed by a month-long break. Most of the students would go home during the breaks. I went back home during my first break. I was so homesick that I wanted to go back home and see my parents, brothers, and sisters, and to report about my new venture. After this first holiday, I did not go back to my village regularly. I stayed at the school to make some money for my schooling. I would supplement what my parents were paying from the fields.

Saturday was work day for us at the school, called general work. Everyone had to work to clean the school grounds, dormitories, and classrooms, from eight in the morning to noon. Each week we would be assigned to different tasks in groups. After lunch, we would use the day as we pleased. Some would go play tennis or soccer, some would study, etc. On Saturday, the students would have what was called "see me time." This was a time when those who wanted would go on dates. I never did go on a date while I was in high school.

After breakfast on Sundays, we would have dormitory cleaning inspection. The faculty member who led the assembly that week would do the inspection. The dormitory that won the cleaning competition would get an award. It was usually some pieces of bread for each member of the winning dorm. After inspection, we would all file in line to go to church in the huge stone church building. Rev. Luke Gurure was the

United Methodist station minister at Murewa Mission at that time. We went to church just as a routine. We did not pay particular attention, nor were we born again.

The Sunday morning service was a combined service with the people in the community. The afternoons were used for social groups like Scripture Union, United Methodist Youth Fellowship, and other groups. When I was in my third year in high school, I was elected as the vice-chairman of the UMYF. I served in this position for one year. I enjoyed serving in this leadership position, but it did not get me closer to the Lord.

My time at Murewa was quite memorable. I made a few friends. I learned many things in those four years. We wrote our final exams at the end of November 1975. These exams were the Cambridge O-Level Exams. I passed all my classes with good grades, but I was not able to go on to Form 5 and 6, which would be the Cambridge Advanced Level. My heart was broken because I could not go on with my education. The bottleneck had gotten me this time. However, I secured a job as a primary school teacher.

CHAPTER 3
TEACHING SCHOOL

At the time when I completed high school, the country was in great need of teachers, especially at the primary level. So they hired young men and women who had passed high school with good grades. I was very happy to be one of the young men hired to teach school. I went to teach in a remote place in Maramba at Guyu School. I was assigned to the grade seven class. I enjoyed teaching, in spite of the fact that the war for independence was escalating during that time. Guyu School was closed because of the war. All the teachers at that school were relocated to different schools in other districts in the third term. I was sent to Kaseke School, where I was assigned to a grade four class. Although Guyu School was closed, the grade seven school students were able to come back and take their grade seven final exams. I was very happy because some of the students whom I taught did very well in the final exams.

I taught at Kaseke for only one term. A term is about three months. The war continued to escalate. One by one the schools were closing. The civilian people were in danger because they were between the freedom fighters and the National Security forces. The freedom fighters demanded that the civilians feed them, and the National Security forces would come to harass the civilians for feeding these men. When it was not safe to stay at Kaseke, I went back to Murewa Mission. I worked in the library and computer lab while I was studying for my Advanced Level courses, in an attempt to proceed to university. I did not have enough sponsorship, so that did not work very well after two semesters. I went back to teaching in the third term of my second year after high school. I was assigned to teach at Rota School, where I taught grade five. I really enjoyed my time at Rota. The students were very keen to learn. In addition to our classroom work, my class staged a play from the Shona book, *Dzasukwa Mwana Asina Hembe* by Patrick Chakaipa, that was presented in front of the whole school. I was elated to be the conducting teacher for the exciting play. One other thing that I liked about being at Rota school was that it was about ten miles from the home that my parents had moved to because of the war, and on some weekends I would walk to go to see them.

After that school term at Rota, I was transferred to Chinhenga School in Mukarakate. Rota School was about three hours walk from where my parents were living. Chinhenga was about four to five hours drive. Untrained teachers had no choice—they were just sent to teach wherever the district needed them. I taught grade four at Chinhenga for one term. I was an industrious teacher. Anywhere that I taught, I tried to be the best I could. At the end of the term there was a turn of events that would change the direction of my life. The war for independence escalated intensely.

One after the other, schools closed. At the end of that first term of the school year, and my first term there, we were told that all schools nationwide, except those which were in the big cities, had to be closed. As schools were closing for the end of that term, we packed our belongings to leave the school for good. I went home to see my family for a short while before quickly moving away to the capital city, Harare, as all the young men and women of age were vacating the rural areas, which were the war zones. One chapter of my life was closing, and another chapter opening.

CHAPTER 4
MOVING TO THE BIG CITY

The two-hour bus ride from my village to the big city took forever to complete. The bus would stop regularly to drop off and pick up passengers. The bus arrived in the city about mid-afternoon. Although I had visited the big city a few times before, the splendor of the city never ceased to amaze me. I was always amazed at how so many people would live and work in such a crowded place. This was in May 1978. Harare is the capital of Zimbabwe. It was called Salisbury then, and the country was called Rhodesia. At that time, the population of the city was less than a million people. Now the city has about two million people or more. As we entered the city, I was amazed to see so many people walking up and down the streets along the pavement. Many cars were driving up and down the busy streets. People were starting to make their way to their homes on public transportation. Significantly fewer people could afford to have their own cars at that time.

When I got off the bus from the village, I went to H. M. Barbour where my cousin, Bernard Nhira, worked. I was a country boy. Maneuvering the streets of the big city was quite a chore to me. I arrived at H. M.

Barbour with a big sigh of relief. Having worked at this business for many years, almost everyone knew who Bernard was. I asked where I could find him, and some workers brought me to his department. He was thrilled to see me. I had to wait for him a while because it was not yet time to get off work. After he finished work, we headed to the buses to go to his house in Mufakose, which would be my home for some months. We had to stand in a long line to get onto the bus. I was amazed at the hustle and bustle of the city life at this hour of the day. I enjoyed the thirty-minute bus ride to my cousin's home. My nephews and nieces were overjoyed at my unexpected arrival. My cousin, his wife, and their children made me feel welcome, and for that I will always be grateful. George, Grace, Eustice, and Brian—my cousin's children—were very accommodating. They helped me fit into their home. I crowded in with them in the boys' bedroom, and they never complained. I stayed with my cousin and his family for six months while I was looking for a job. Jobs were not easy to come by. Just as today as at that time, many young people had vacated the rural areas, which were war zones, to find refuge in the big cities.

A few days after I had arrived in Harare, I started looking for employment. I did not know where to start. In an attempt to go overseas for further education, I had sent my O-Level original certificate, without making a copy, to my Uncle Alois Mangwende, who was working and studying overseas. Wherever I tried to go find work, they would ask for an O-Level certificate, and I would tell them that I had one, but I had sent it to Britain, where I was applying for further studies. That did not help me at all. Eventually an acquaintance found me a job selling newspapers at the bus stop. For a month or so, I sold newspapers at a bus stop in Mufakose. Although that did not bring in much money, I enjoyed the opportunity of waking up early in the morning to do something. I remember one day that somebody took the newspaper and boarded the bus without paying. I climbed on the bus after him, and I almost got knocked off by the bus conductor, and I ended up with some bruises.

During this time, I would visit my sister Charity, who was living with Aunt Christine Chikore. They would assure me that I would get a job someday, but I needed to give my life to Christ. This would irritate me. Each time I came over, this would be the same conversation that they would have with me. I was really bothered about it.

CHAPTER 5
BORN AGAIN

When my sister Charity started sharing about the born-again experience, I was irritated; however, God started speaking to my heart. I started to ask myself questions. Who I am? Where did I come from? Where am I going? Who made me? These questions puzzled me. I started thinking about this born-again experience that they were sharing with me. Charity was staying with our Aunt Christine Chikore in Kambuzuma in Harare. Charity had also left the village because of the difficulties that young people were facing in the rural areas at that time. While she was staying in Kambuzuma, she received Jesus Christ as her Lord and personal Savior. Also she was healed of a large goiter that had grown on her neck. She began to share enthusiastically about the saving and healing power of Christ with everybody she came in contact with.

I would visit her and our aunt in Kambuzuma from Mufakose, which was about five miles away. Each time I came, they would talk to me and encourage me that I was going to get a job one day. They were adamant that I needed to receive Christ before that would happen. Week after week they would share the

Jesus experience. I would put up my defense: the fact that I did not need that philosophy. The more I heard them, the more I felt troubled as to what I needed to do about this. Some of my thoughts said that these were only illusions. Some of my thoughts said that it was truth. My sister kept inviting me to visit her church. I kept postponing.

Finally, to get this lady off my back, I decided to go to church with them one Sunday morning. I walked the five-mile trip from Mufakose to Kambuzuma with apprehension. I arrived at Aunt Christine's house early that morning. Their house was next to the church they attended, Kambuzuma Ezekiel Chapel. When it was time for church, we walked into the chapel.

The service began with songs of praise and worship. It was a different atmosphere than I had ever experienced in a church service. At the preaching of the Word of God, I listened intently. The Word of God was convicting and convincing. I tried to reason out why one should not believe these things. The Spirit of the Lord convinced me that I needed to be saved. I was convinced that I was a sinner and I needed salvation. When the preacher gave the altar call asking for those who wanted to receive Christ to come forward, I jumped out of my seat and went to the front. I do not even remember who the preacher was. A few of us went up. We stood up front waiting to be prayed for. The preacher led us through the salvation prayer. After he led us through the prayer, I felt something like a log fall off my shoulders. My body felt lighter than I had ever felt. I felt relieved. I was filled with joy unspeakable. We were congratulated by the preacher and the congregation for entering the kingdom of God. I went back to my cousin Bernard with great joy. This was in September 1978.

After I gavc my life to Christ, I became hungry for the Word of God. I started attending the Mufakose Assembly of God Africa Church, which was about a mile from my cousin's house where I lived. I would not miss a service. At home, I would wake up early in the morning to read a Bible that I had been given. I would devour the book. One day in a prayer service, I felt something come on me like a wave of electricity. I did not know what it was. Someone told me it was the Holy Spirit's anointing that had come on me.

A few weeks later in a church service, the preacher who spoke in the afternoon service preached about the baptism of the Holy Spirit. At the end of her sermon, she asked people who wanted to receive the Holy Spirit to come forward. A group of us went to the front. She prayed for us by laying hands on us. I remember that when she laid hands on me that I was slain in the Spirit. I fell on the floor of that United Methodist Church building that they rented for afternoon services. I lay there for over an hour praying in tongues. When I came back to myself, all the people were gone except two deacons who were closing up the building. A few months later, I was baptized in water in a nearby stream, along with several others. I was filled with great joy at what was happening in my life. A new chapter had started in my life.

One brother in that church became my "Barnabas". If ever I missed a service, Dabson would come to visit me and find out how I was doing. In those early days, my faith was tested. Dabson was there for me. Sometimes when he came to check on me, I would hide in the bathroom, and I would tell my nephews to tell him that I was not home. But Dabson would not give up on me. He would come back another time and another time, until my faith grew stronger. A few weeks after I received Jesus Christ as my Savior, I got a job at the Textbook Sales Book Center in Harare. Uncle Sherman Chikore was responsible for this job offer because he was one of the managers there. After I got the job, they also arranged for me to move from Mufakose to Kambuzuma, so that I would be close to them and they could watch me grow in the Lord. The Chikores lived in Kambuzuma Section 2, and I lodged in one room in Section 4 with a family from the church.

CHAPTER 6
WORKING AT TEXTBOOK SALES BOOK CENTER AND STANDARD CHARTERED BANK

Uncle Sherman Chikore was one of the managers at the Textbook Sales Book Center in downtown Harare. When I got saved, he was very enthusiastic to find me employment with his company because he knew that I qualified for some position there. He worked with the sales department, and the vacancy that had opened up was in the accounts department at the light industrial site. I was assigned to the debtors department.

It was a great joy to be able to have a job where I woke up every morning anticipating a day's work and expecting a paycheck at the end of the month. However, I worked with some guys who used the filthiest language that I had never heard before. I determined that I was not going to follow suit. I used my lunch breaks to read my Bible. I fasted often. I remember one time when I was attempting to fast forty days. I was taking one meal a day after work. When I had fasted twenty-eight days, there was such opposition at my work place that I did not know what to do. After a Sunday service, the denominational leader of our church then counseled me, and asked me to quit fasting and to start at another time. That was wise counsel. I broke the fast. After that, in my thirty years as a Christian, I have fasted forty days at four different times.

In July 1979, I was conscripted for national service. I spent ten months in Bulawayo working for the government. The only time I came back to Harare during that time was when my sister got married to Fabian Chigome, in December 1979. On April 18, 1980, Rhodesia gained indepdence, and it became Zimbabwe. The war for independence ended. I went back to Harare. My friends and family were so happy to see me back in Harare. When I went back to Textbook Sales, though, they told me that they had downsized, and that my job was no longer available.

While I was in Bulawayo, I had written my uncle in London to help me get my O-Level original certificate (which I had sent by mistake when I was applying for further studies). He had tracked it down and found it, and he sent it back to me. Because I had good O-Level grades, I applied and got a job with Standard Chartered Bank in July 1980. I was assigned to the branch on Robert Mugabe and First Street. I lodged in a room at Rev. and Mrs. Cuthbert Makoni's home in Westwood, Harare. I thoroughly enjoyed my job at the bank. I worked in the correspondence department, foreign exchange department, and savings department during the two years that I worked for the bank.

I was so on fire for God. At the bank, the accountant and I would get together for Bible study in the lunch room. I was blessed to be a member of a church that knew how to pray. We would fast every Monday for the whole day, and we met at the church for intense prayer from 6:00 pm to 8:00 pm. The church would be packed for prayer, and the Spirit would be moving. I became a member of the youth group of the church, as well as another group of young people called Revival Band. The Revival Band was led by my friend Noah Sargent. In December 1981, the Revival Band team went to my parents' Nhira Village in Murewa District to preach the gospel. I had written to my father telling him how I had received Christ, and that I wanted him saved, too. He obliged and allowed me to bring a group of our youth team to come and preach the gospel. On a Friday, Saturday, and Sunday, we had a weekend of spiritual fire in the village. My father and many others got saved that weekend, and a church was started in my parents' home.

CHAPTER 7
THE LOVE OF MY LIFE

It was at the beginning of 1981 when my pastor, Bishop Patterson Ngorima, asked when I was going to be married. I disdained that question very much. I was not ready to be married. I told him it might be in about four more years. Words are powerful. When he asked me that question, it began to linger in my mind. The church that I was a part of was strong in fasting and praying. We were taught to pray and fast. Beginning in 1980, I had started the practice of fasting three days and three nights once a month, in addition to every Monday when the whole church fasted and prayed.

One Saturday morning, I went to work at my job at Standard Chartered Bank in downtown Harare. When I arrived that morning, I found that it was not my day to work (we rotated Saturdays in my department). Instead of going back home, I went to the Anglican Cathedral, which was always open for prayer during the day. I was on my second day of three days of prayer and fasting. When I got in the church, it was all quiet and no one was in the building. I picked a good place to kneel down and pray. A little while into the prayer, I saw a vision in my mind. In the vision there were five girls from my church standing in front of me. Four of the young ladies disappeared, and one young lady remained standing in front of me. I became very emotional and started crying. I told the Lord, "If you want me to marry Constance, I will do it." In that emotional state, I continued to pray until the burden was lifted; then I left to go home.

I had found the love of my life. I kept the vision to myself without telling anyone anything for a few weeks. I felt drawn to this beautiful young lady. It was pleasurable just to look at her each time when we went to church. We were part of the youth group and a select group that used to go out to evangelize our community under street lights. I never shared with anyone what was on my heart about this lady, but I was blessed just to glance at her at church or at Revival Band meetings.

Several weeks after seeing the vision, I decided to go tell my pastor what was in my heart. I told him that I had found a girl whom I liked. In my church at that time, one did not just go out and approach a girl for a date. We had to go to the leaders of the church to talk to a girl about getting in love. Therefore, my pastor arranged the meeting so we could talk. We met at the pastor's home in the living room. I asked her if we could be married. She said, "If the Lord has shown you that, let it be so."

A month later, our pastor announced our engagement in church. The day when it was announced that Constance and I had fallen in love was a historic day for us and the church. There was such joyful wailing, whistling, and shouting that the whole community around the church wondered what had happened. A few months later, Constance and a friend, along with a few of my relatives, visited my parents in the village in Murewa. Later we visited Constance's aunt in Gutu. Six months after the announcement, I sent my Uncle Shadreck Nhira to take the *lobola*, or dowry, to my prospective in-laws. The process went smoothly, and we were granted permission to get married.

In our culture, the bridegroom is responsible for paying for the wedding. So it was my responsibility to pay for all that the wedding needed. It never bothered me a bit because I was so excited to get my bride. The wedding came about ten months after our engagement, on May 1, 1982. Our wedding took the whole day. It was indeed an exciting day. Over two hundred relatives and friends packed the church in Kambuzuma to celebrate our wedding. Our marriage officer, Rev. Michael Maoko, was so overjoyed that after we recited our vows, he forgot to ask the bridegroom to kiss his wife. I had never kissed Constance during the ten months of dating. I had been looking forward to this. Nevertheless, on our way to our honeymoon, I kissed my wife for the first time in our elder's car while going to the Jameson Hotel. We did have the time of our lives.

CHAPTER 8
THE CALL

Ten days after our wedding, the Lord sent Constance and me to a Bible school in Harare. A few months before our marriage, the Lord had been dealing with me to leave my job at Standard Chartered Bank to go into the ministry. This sparked some controversy because some from the church were in favor and several were not at all in favor, including some of the leaders of our church.

Some even offered to find me another job, if I were fed up with working in the bank. One of the key elders of the church that we were a part of took the time to explain to me the kind of life that pastors lived. He told me it was a life of poverty because pastors were not paid enough. My parents, particularly my father, were not at all happy with the decision. Ultimately, he let me make the decision, even though he expressed his disapproval. I knew what the Lord had been saying, so I decided to follow the vision that God had given to me. I resigned my bank job two weeks before our marriage. Ten days after our wedding, we packed our few belongings to go to a small Bible school in Glen Norah on the outskirts of Harare.

Several things led to the call. Soon after I gave my life to Christ, I became a part of a church in Kambuzuma which was on fire for God. Prayer was a way of life for most of the people in this church. Once in a while I would take young men from the church for all-night prayer on a hill near the suburb. At church, I would not miss any prayer meeting times. Monday was fasting and prayer day at the church. I would always make sure that I was there an hour before the meeting began. I would lie down under the benches, praying in the Spirit. On Friday nights and Sunday nights, I would go out with a group of young people who were on fire for God, and we would sing and preach Jesus under a street light. The Lord used this group of young people to bring many into the kingdom and into the house of God.

CHAPTER 9
AT AFRICA MULTINATION FOR CHRIST INSTITUTE

It was easy to move to the Bible school. We did not have many belongings. One load took all that we had in a small truck to the Bible school, which was a few miles from Westwood, Kambuzuma, where I had just started a new life with my new bride. However, the difficult part was detaching ourselves from the people whom we had learned to love: our friends and family from Kambuzuma Ezekiel Chapel. It took us several weeks to part with our folks in our minds.

Our belongings all fit in one small room. The living room and bedroom were all in that small room. The kitchen was in one corner of that small room. We ate most of our meals in the school cafeteria. The food was mostly cabbage, beans, and sadza (a cooked cornmeal dish). The call was so strong that we never saw this as a problem. Once in a while we would go the store to buy meat. After Constance became pregnant, two months after our wedding, she had more frequent cravings for meat. We always looked to God to provide. Every so often He did.

Once we got to the school, we started to pray early-morning prayers. We went to the school chapel to pray almost every day around five o'clock in the morning. There would be a few other students in the chapel praying as well. A couple of years before getting married, I had developed the habit of fasting three days and three nights once a month. I continued this practice when we got to the Bible school. One time after three days of prayer and fasting, another student, an elderly gentleman, came to me and said, "Your face is shining, what's wrong with you?" I did not know what to tell him. However, this was confirmation of what God was doing inside and outside my life. I continued the fasting three days and three nights for twenty years.

The Bible school was small, but we learned a lot. There were close to a hundred students at that time. We went to school from morning to lunch time. After lunch, we went to do general work on the campus. I was assigned to start classes for those who wanted to develop their reading and writing skills. The classes were given at night. I would use the afternoon to plan, prepare, and grade the students' work. At the end of the second year at the Bible school, some of the students were able to sit for their Zimbabwe Junior Certificate and passed. Constance and I transitioned out at the end of our second year at the Bible school.

CHAPTER 10
PASTORING

While we were at the Bible school, we began to feel fire in our bones. We were not able just to stay in class. So we started to call pastors to go and preach for them. Most weekends we were on the road preaching around the churches in Harare. In my second year at Bible school, I started traveling with evangelistic teams that were going to villages and small towns outside Harare. A time or two while I was at the school, I led a team of evangelists in two tent crusades, and I planted two churches. At the end of our second year, we moved to a church for our first pastorate.

The overseer of the Harare Province assigned us to go and pastor the Tafara Assembly of God Church. This church had been known for running pastors out of town. We breathed a sigh of amazement at the working of the Lord. We summoned our faith to go and face that congregation. We were "green" from Bible school. Some of the people whom we were going to pastor were our parents' age. They had never been pastored by such novices. They had a history of being pastored by notables in the denomination. When we arrived at Tafara, we could see faces showing amazement at what the denominational leaders had decided to send them. Nevertheless, they received us in compliance with what the elders of the church had decided. Their faces, however, were saying, "Let's see what is going to happen here."

We went to Tafara Assembly in December 1983. In February 1984, we were ordained with the Zimbabwe Assemblies of God Africa. The Holy Spirit went ahead of us to Tafara Assembly. There was such calmness at the church when we arrived. The leaders and the church welcomed us beyond our expectation. We prayed and fasted for the Holy Spirit to continue working. The church came together as never before. We exhorted the church to move on and to expand the kingdom of God in that community. Everybody developed a mind to work. We developed home Bible study groups, which became the keys to the growth of that church. We had ladies home prayer groups and Bible study groups. In less than two years, the church doubled in attendance.

The evil one was not sleeping while we were doing all this. He was provoked by the growth of the church and the unity of the body. He stirred some in the church to create havoc within the body. We realized that it was the work of the devil himself. We called the church to corporate prayer. The ones who were involved in the disturbances did not participate. The leadership of the church and some of the key people in the church told us to step back. They took it upon themselves, and they said that they were going to handle the matter themselves. Constance and I kept on praying and fasting from the background. The leaders talked to the people who were causing havoc. Within a few weeks there was calm again in the church. The church became united again. They loved us again, and as always, we continued to love them. The church bought us a brand new set of furniture. At the end of our second year, we were transferred to Waterfalls, Harare.

It was a December day, while we were going through the routine of our tasks at Tafara, when the church truck arrived at the pastor's house where we had lived for two years. The driver informed us that the leadership of the church had decided that we were to move to Waterfalls. We made a few phones calls to the leaders of Tafara Assembly. Some of them came to the pastor's house immediately. Before long, there was a small congregation in the pastor's house, praying and crying that perhaps there would be a change and we would be allowed to stay. The truck driver waited for things to calm down. After a while, the leaders of the church saw that they were wasting their time. So they got out of the way and let the movers do their work. Within a few hours, we were all packed up and ready to move to our next assignment.

Waterfalls Assembly was like a resting place. The church people there were very calm and somewhat reserved. We fell in love with the church, and the church with us. Most of the people there minded their own business. The growth of this church was not as dramatic as the previous church, although we saw some growth during the one year that we were at Waterfalls. We lived in the same building as the archbishop and founder of the Zimbabwe Assemblies of God for several months because he was awaiting the building of his own house in one of the low-density suburbs. We each minded our own business, and the two families lived quiet lives. We probably made some noise because we had some younger children growing up, but our neighbors did not complain.

The Archbishop met me on the grounds of the new headquarters of the church, and he announced to me, "I am going to send you very far." In a few days the church truck was ready for us. A pastor friend and I were moved to Chiredzi and Masvingo on the same day. The truck dropped my family at Mucheke in Masvingo, and then proceeded to deliver the other family farther away in Chiredzi. We both had been involved in the Harare Minister's Fraternal. The church in Masvingo had been involved in some upheavals. It was chaotic at the church, and they did not know how to receive us. As before, the Holy Spirit had gone before us. We experienced unexpected calm.

We prayed for the unity of the church. We got the church involved in prayer as well. As we had done in Tafara, we formed effective home Bible study groups and ladies prayer groups. Within a year, there was such a sweet spirit within the church. In the second year, the church doubled in attendance. It became the talk of the town. Another reason for the growth of this church was developing leaders. We had several regional elders, and under them we had deacons. We patterned our church after the early church of Acts 2. We began to see great growth. At Tafara and

Mucheke, the pastors' houses were very old. One of the veteran leaders of the denomination said that the Tafara house was like a witchdoctor's house. At Mucheke, when all the issues of the church had been settled, we decided to build a new pastor's house, which we never lived in because we moved to our next assignment, as the Lord was leading.

During our second year of pastoring in Tafara, I had the great opportunity to travel to the country of Zambia, our neighbor to the north. The church officials in the headquarter offices picked me to go on official business to the church in Zambia. Fire was burning in my bones, and I offered to go at any time. In that year, I travelled a total of six times to Lusaka and Ndola. While I was on these missions, I got to preach in crusades in different locations in those cities. I also got to speak in some of their big Sunday services. I enjoyed preaching the gospel in Zambia. I saw many people saved, as well as many healed by the power of God.

When we were at Mucheke I was sent to Botswana to help the church there start home Bible study groups. I was there for about two weeks. I met with the pastor and the leadership of the church several times. We started a few home groups.

I had been transferred from Waterfalls, Harare, to "far away" Mucheke, Masvingo, because of participating in the Harare Ministers' Fraternal. When we got to Masvingo, I looked for the ministerial fellowship of the city. I was so happy to see ministers from different denominations who met together once a month. I believed that if we were to change our city that we would have to unite as a ministerial body. No one denomination could do it alone. I strongly believe that there are people in the Catholic Church, Methodist Church, Lutheran Church, Baptist Church, Assemblies of God Church, and many other denominational groups going to heaven. To win many others, we must work together. In our second year in Masvingo, I was elected the president of the Masvingo Ministers' Fraternal. While I was president, we sought out other ministers from different churches, and the fellowship started to grow bigger. We conducted a citywide all-churches gathering in one of the biggest halls in the city of Masvingo. What a gathering of joy we had!

CHAPTER 11
ADMINISTERING A SCHOOL

When I gave my life to Christ, I did not give up my passion for education. After I started working at Textbook Sales Book Center, I enrolled to do my A-Level studies with Rapid Results College. I was not able to balance my time at work, at church, and with my studies, so my studies did not go very smoothly. I quit studying for a while, and I focused on growing up in the Lord.

An opportunity arose, however, to be involved in education. Zimbabwe Assemblies of God Africa wanted to start a Christian school. They looked for someone to get this project off the ground. A year before I got married, I got involved with the school project. We started a study group, which offered classes for Form 1 to Form 4. I was the administrator of the school. I hired teachers and advertised the school for students to come. The school grew to the point where the government began to pay our teachers. One of the teachers was my brother, Tafadzwa Nhira. The school produced quality graduates. I meet some of them who are doing some wonderful work for the Lord and their communities.

When I went to Bible school, I continued to work with the school. I started an academic school, which met at the Bible school in the evening. We also helped start a school of dressmaking and a school of cookery. Many churches in Zimbabwe now offer dressmaking classes. While pastoring at Tafara, Waterfalls, and Mucheke, I continued to be administrator of the school. From Masvingo, I would come once a month to monitor and to meet with teachers. The schools continued to flourish after I left for my next assignment.

CHAPTER 12
MOVING TO AMERICA VIA CHRIST FOR THE NATIONS INSTITUTE

We were in our second year at Mucheke in Masvingo when I got a stirring to further my studies. I wrote to a friend who was at Christ for the Nations Institute in Dallas, Texas, to send me an application. I submitted my application. I received the greatest news of my life when I got the letter from CFNI saying that I had been accepted into their one-year Christian Leadership program. I was given a work-study scholarship. I would go to school in the morning and work on campus in the afternoon, Monday through Friday. My wife Constance was elated that her husband would leave to go to school in America. Through her job as a dressmaking teacher at the church where we were pastoring, she helped me to raise the money for the airline ticket.

My journey to America was my first airplane ride ever. I was anxious, but I encouraged myself that many people had flown and that I could do it, too. My flight was from Harare to Lilongwe to Amsterdam, then to Atlanta, Georgia. Atlanta was my port of entry. After clearing immigration and customs, I then flew to the Dallas-Fort Worth Airport. I hired a shuttle to take me to the campus of Christ for the Nations Institute. I had left Harare on December 23, 1988, and I arrived at CFNI on December 24, the day before Christmas.

My first Christmas in America was quite different from what I had known. In Zimbabwe, I was used to going to church on Christmas day. I was away from my family for the first time in a long time. Some acquaintances from Zimbabwe who had heard that I had come to CFNI came over to get me on Christmas day. We visited until the day was over. During the next few days, I familiarized myself with the campus. Soon after the new year, the campus—which had been quiet because everybody had gone for the winter break—began to buzz again. Before long, school started. There were about a thousand students, plus faculty and staff.

I applied myself at CFNI. I sat close to the front in every one of my classes. To tell the truth, I had a difficult time understanding the Texas accent. They had an even more difficult time understanding me when I spoke. So the first couple months, it was a little hard for me to adjust. A friend encouraged me by telling me that everyone, no matter who you are suffers, from homesickness. I missed my wife and two little children, Proper and Jasper, terribly. I would talk to my wife once or twice a month.

There was no telephone in the house where we lived in Mucheke. So she had to go with the children and sleep at the home of one of the deacons for me to call early the next morning. During one of our conversations on the phone, I promised Constance that I would never go away from her or let her go away like I had done. During these conversations, I would talk to Constance and each of the children. We were about 8,000 miles away from each other—Dallas to Harare. During one of the phone calls, my son Jasper asked me, "Dad, where are you? When are you coming home?" I broke down because of that. However, I strengthened myself.

My time at Christ for the Nations was very productive. I applied myself in all my classes, and I worked hard at the work assignments. My main task was cleaning the Institute Building where chapel was held and where some of the bigger classes met. I vacuumed the building and cleaned the restrooms. Along with others, we cleaned it the best we could. During the weekends, I spent many hours in prayer in the Gordon Lindsay Tower prayer room. I can say that my time at CFNI was very fruitful. It was a great time to anchor my life and ministry. I learned many things both in the classes and out of the classes.

Christ for the Nations Institute had a Sunday afternoon service. Sunday mornings, all students were required to go to a church of their choice in the Dallas-Fort Worth area. Some students went to "church on the pillow"—they slept in. A friend of mine, Noah Sajeni, who had graduated from CFNI, introduced me to a great pastor who pastored at Emmanuel Christian Center, Rev. Edgar Terrell. He was a wonderful shepherd of his flock. Each Sunday morning he would come to CFNI campus to pick up a carload of students to go to his church. The church was a small, but very friendly and loving. We bonded with the church members—they loved us and we loved them. Later on, we were ordained with Christ for the Nations Fellowship of Ministers and Churches.

CHAPTER 13
STEP OF FAITH TO ORAL ROBERTS UNIVERSITY

In my full year at Christ for the Nations, I only missed one day of school. That day was the Friday when I left to go to visit the campus of Oral Roberts University in Tulsa, Oklahoma, during their college weekend. I spent the night traveling on a Greyhound bus, arriving in Tulsa in the morning. My friend picked me up from the bus station, and he took me to his house to shower and have a hot breakfast. I participated in the college for a weekend that Friday and Saturday. On Sunday morning, I left to go back to Dallas. I had not seen such a beautiful college campus. The atmosphere was so attractive. Watching all the students walking around the campus in ties and some in jackets was so captivating. I knew that I was supposed to go to ORU. However, how to go was the issue.

I did not know how it would happen for me to attend ORU. I did not have the money nor the sponsors to attend. Inside, though, I knew that I was supposed to be there. So I started the application process. I got stuck on the financing part. Another issue was that CFNI wanted me to return home, as had been stated in my visa. However, if I were fully accepted at ORU, then I would legally extend my visa status. The process to change the visa status was longer than the time that I had. I trusted God that all would take place according to His will. I was fully persuaded that I would go to ORU.

I was not yet accepted to attend ORU, and I did not have a return ticket to go back to Zimbabwe. Through the prompting of the Holy Spirit, a friend of mine—Mike Holman from the Lancaster, Texas, area—loaned me money to buy airline tickets for my wife and two children to come to America (which I was able to repay a few years later). December graduation at Christ for the Nations Institute came. I still was in limbo. My attempt to get visas for my family to come proved impossible. They were supposed to come right after my graduation from CFNI. They could not come. I did not know what to do next. I talked to another friend, Michael Ntou from Ghana, about hosting me after graduation. I stayed with Michael the whole winter break. He was a great host. During the time that I was at his house, I sought the Lord in prayer and fasting, asking the Lord's mind and His favor to move.

I left Dallas a few days before New Year's day. The Lord moved on Mike Holman to give me $500 to go and start school at ORU. Five hundred was very little money compared to the amount that was needed for school, but I had something in my hand to get started. Paul and Shirley Chapinduka were gracious to offer me a place to stay in their apartment at the graduate housing on the ORU campus. I stayed with them for a few weeks while I was getting myself situated. I talked with people at church and everywhere about my situation of needing financial help, but the doors seemed closed. The university administrators saw that I was determined to get into school, and they gave me a chance. I was offered a work-study job on campus to clean the fourth floor of the Graduate Center. I found an apartment of my own. The school found me some scholarships to get started. The favor of the Lord was working with me. I got validated a few weeks after everyone else. The next move was to get my family over from Zimbabwe.

CHAPTER 14
FAMILY FOLLOWS TO AMERICA

Constance had stayed at the Forward in Faith Church in Mucheke, Masvingo, when I left to go to America. The hierarchy of the church was very gracious to us, and they asked her to stay and pastor the church that we had been pastoring together. The church had continued to grow. She proved to be a great pastor. After months of calling each other once or twice a month, Constance and our daughter Prosper and son Jasper were finally able to follow me to America.

As mentioned earlier, my friend Mike Holman loaned us money for their airline tickets. They were to come in December, right after my graduation from CFNI. It took weeks for them to receive the visas to come to America. Several times they were denied the legal papers to fly out. Meanwhile they were asked by the church to vacate the church house for a new pastor to come and fill our place. Stranded with nowhere to go, Constance asked the church to deliver our belongings to the village in Murewa. She and the children went to her brother, Flavian Zinyemba, to wait for the visas. They stayed there for three months before the breakthrough came. It was agonizing to go to the American Embassy several times and to be denied a visa. In another way, though, it was a blessing in disguise. Had they come while I was a student at CFNI, they would not have had a place to stay. Even if they had come during my early days at ORU, they would have suffered also with no real place to lodge. After I had settled into my own apartment, one day Constance was summoned to the US Embassy to get their visas. Praise the Lord! Before, they had gathered all the relatives and friends to celebrate their departure for America the next day, but they were denied visas. This time, the day after they were granted visas, they left without telling anybody except the immediate family. Constance told them to tell everybody after they had landed in the States.

Constance and the children thoroughly enjoyed their plane rides. They flew from Harare to Heathrow Airport in London, then to Atlanta, Georgia. After processing through immigration and customs, they landed at the Dallas-Fort Worth Airport in Texas. It was amazing how they were able to maneuver their way through the airline transit. The kids enjoyed the trip so much. They were able to go see the pilot in the cockpit. They were given goody bags to play with on the plane ride: crayons, coloring books, airplane pins, and other items. I was waiting eagerly to see my family after fifteen months. My friend Paul had driven me from Tulsa to Dallas to pick up the family. When their plane landed my heart began to pound as they were taking so long to clear immigration and customs. Finally they came out! I was beside myself. I hugged and kissed Constance. I picked up Prosper and kissed her. Then I picked up Jasper and kissed him.

Everybody around stopped to stare at us. My friend Paul was taking pictures during this ecstatic moment. It took a while for this to settle down. Was there not a cause for such jubilation? Being away from each other made us grow fonder. We drove to CFNI to show them the campus. After seeing the campus and some friends nearby, we left for Tulsa, Oklahoma. We had a great trip to Tulsa, talking, laughing, and rejoicing over this great reunion. Before we knew it, we arrived in Tulsa before midnight.

That week in our new home was a reunion week. We ran around with the kids putting them in school. We picked them up on Saturday. Sunday we were in church at Victory Christian Center in Tulsa, which would become our home church for three years. I never missed one day of school except the day our younger son Brian was born. It took us several weeks to develop a routine. For me, the routine was going to school early in the morning. After school, I would go to work on campus until late in the evening. Then I would go home to see the family for a little while before doing assignments and going to sleep. On Saturdays, I went to work and to study in the school library. Sundays, we went to church as a family, and soon after church I went to work. This became my routine for the first four years at ORU. It helped me graduate debt-free with my first degree, a BA in Evangelism.

CHAPTER 15
PLUGGING IN

Before my family came, I visited a few churches in the Tulsa area. Friends would come to take me to church. I also went to the nearby church, which was less than a mile away from my apartment. I could walk to church services. This church also sent out buses to pick up people from their neighborhoods to take to church. Victory Christian Center was bigger than any church that I had pastored or attended. The church was full of life. The pastors were friendly. When I met them for the first time, they were like I had met them before. The preaching was powerful. The singing was like I had never heard before. The first time in service, I was very impressed. After praise and worship, the whole church, about 7,000 people in that morning service, got to pray for one another. We introduced ourselves to each other first, and then we shared prayer requests. In leading us to pray for each other, the pastor said, "There are VIPs on either side, in front of you, and behind you. Introduce yourself and pray for them." WOW! I had never heard of that. We introduced ourselves and we prayed for each other. I requested prayer for my family to come to America. The whole place was charged with fervent prayer and faith. From that moment I was encouraged that my family was going to come and join me.

When my family joined me on March 16, 1990, I never had any problem with where to go to church. I had already picked a church when they arrived. We were going to be part of Victory Christian Center. It was just logical that we were to go there because of its proximity to where we lived. We could walk or ride a church bus. The church that met on the campus of ORU where I worked, even on weekends, was the right one for us. Our search for a church stopped immediately. We enjoyed the singing, the preaching, and the friends that we met each Sunday. Pastor Billy Joe Daugherty was a great preacher. Pastor Sharon Daugherty was a wonderful singer and preacher, too. Her love for God and people is contagious; she never meets a stranger. I also participated in a cell group. I always enjoyed the times when I got to go to the prayer room for prayer. We quickly got plugged in. The various activities at the church kept us involved, and we enjoyed that. I was one of the very first people to go and work voluntarily at Camp Victory when that property was given to the church. We enjoyed growing in the Lord there. Our children enjoyed the children's ministry there. We had found a home away from home. The only difference was that we missed the intimacy that we had with the small church of 200 people that we pastored in Zimbabwe. It did not affect us too much, though, because we were not the pastors here.

Our children enjoyed Victory. However, as time went on, they became disgruntled because there were so many kids and they could not participate effectively in the kids' services. After three years at Victory, we saw our kids drawing back. As father and mother, of course, we had to go to church and so did the kids. But we noticed that they were not as happy as they were before. We tried to find out why, and they told us that they were not involved in the kids' activities in the way they wanted because there were too many kids. At ORU, one of my professors invited Pastor Jonathan Wakefield to speak in one of the classes. I learned that Pastor Wakefield had a church that met across the street from ORU in the Grandview Hotel. The next Sunday, we visited the church. It was a very small church of about fifty or less. Our kids, however, enjoyed the service. The teachers enjoyed our children, and our children thoroughly enjoyed this small church. In 1993, we started going to Harvest Church Assembly of God. The church was small, but we enjoyed participating in the services. Three years after we joined Harvest Church, the church moved from the Grandview to the former Joy Lutheran facility, three miles south, which Harvest had purchased.

One thing that our family especially liked about Harvest Church was that it was small, and we had the opportunity to participate in services. We did miss Victory, the singing, the preaching, the cell groups, and the friendships that we had made. Harvest Church, though, would be the church that helped us get our green cards. Through Pastor Wakefield, we were able to connect with several pastors who would invite us to their churches to preach, as we started our travelling ministry that year. Pastor Wakefield had spent over nineteen years in Africa with his missionary parents, David and Claudia Wakefield. His personality attracted many international students. Later, I was nominated to the Board of Trustees for Harvest Church. The children later returned to be members of Victory where they had made more friends. Constance and I remained affiliated with Harvest Church. We are also members of the Victory Leadership Network.

CHAPTER 16
PRESIDENT OF THE AFRICAN CHRISTIAN FELLOWSHIP TULSA CHAPTER

A few months after I arrived in Tulsa, I felt the need to gather with people from the continent of Africa. I was told that there had been an African fellowship, but that it had quit meeting. I checked to see who had been involved and what they were thinking about it. I came across a brother from Nigeria, who was an Oral Roberts University student then, Ibinabo Dick. He actually had been one of the founders of the African Christian Fellowship USA. The Tulsa chapter of the ACF had been the headquarter chapter for a number of years, but it had become defunct. Ibinabo gave me the encouragement to get it started. We gathered a few people together for our first meeting, who could fit into a small living room of a university housing apartment. There was nothing like fellowshipping with people from the same continent.

When we met, we would sing some of the songs that we sang back home. Some of our speakers would preach like the people from back home. We would pray like we used to pray in Africa. We chose a Friday night that we could spend the whole night in prayer.

At the beginning of the year, we would fast and pray and gather for prayer each night for ten days. We would choose a home, and sometimes rotate homes, and pray night after night. It was wonderful to see God answer our prayers. College students would enter into this time of prayer and would see God miraculously provide for their college tuition balances.

A year after I became president of the ACF Tulsa chapter, we arranged a trip to Washington DC for the national ACF convention. There were hundreds of people, mostly African diaspora. We rented a fifteen-seat van, which was filled to capacity with several of the Tulsa chapter members. The trip from Tulsa to Washington DC took us thirty-one hours. It was summer time, and it did not seem that long because of the joy that we had among ourselves. The four-day conference was so exciting, and the days went by so fast. We came back very encouraged by the wonderful speakers who were at the ACF convention. As a nucleus body of ACF members in Tulsa, we came back knit together, setting the stage for continuity. I led the fellowship for two years, 1991 and 1992. Those were very exciting years for me and my wife. Leading the fellowship rejuvenated the gift of pastoring, which had been lying dormant after two years of focusing on school. At the leading of the Lord, I handed the reigns of leadership to another leader, as I entered into a different ministry.

CHAPTER 17
BEGINNING A TRAVELING MINISTRY IN AMERICA

Having been a pastor for five years in Zimbabwe, it was difficult to sit in class for four years without preaching. Including the time when I preached in my homiletics class, I could count about four times of preaching. It was like a prison for me. While at ORU in 1993, in my third year as an undergraduate student, a door opened for me to go to Jamaica on a Spring Break mission trip by myself. A friend, who had been my dorm-mate at CFNI, invited me to come to Montego Bay, Jamaica. Eugene and Lisa Staton were teaching at the CFNI Jamaica campus. They hosted me at the campus, and they arranged wonderful meetings, including one of the greatest churches in that area, on the campus, and in one of the villages. It was indeed an exciting mission.

When I returned from the Jamaican mission trip, I found amazing developments. I had helped my young brother, Tafadzwa, come to America to attend ORU. He was a hard worker and he worked his way through school. This particular time was his first semester. It was during Spring Break, and he had been working in the school cafeteria. The college was hosting a missions conference. During the conference, Tafadzwa met some delegates from Mound City, Kansas: Jane Marcum and Shirley Williams. Tafadzwa and the two visitors liked each other, and they got to talking. He shared about his brother, who was a preacher and was traveling in Jamaica on his Spring Break. The ladies invited Tafadzwa and his brother to come to Kansas. Upon learning about this invitation when I returned from Jamaica, we made arrangements to go up to Kansas in a few weeks.

A few weeks after my return from Jamaica, my wife Constance, our three children, and my brother Tafadzwa drove up to Mound City, Kansas, for our first ministry trip in America. It was a four-hour drive up north of Tulsa. We stayed at a guest house called Shalom. John and Grace Rieder were the hosts of this beautiful guest home. We had not met such an exciting couple. They had been missionaries in Ivory Coast for over thirty years. They had lived in Africa for so long that when they said, "Our people," they meant the people of Ivory Coast. They were now ministering in the States by hosting groups that came to have conferences at Shalom. That weekend we preached at a conference that was being held there. That Sunday, we preached at two churches in the morning: Liberty Church and Cornerstone. This would be the beginning of our traveling ministry in the United States.

A few weeks later, we returned to Mound City to preach in the same churches. This time Constance had been asked to be the speaker of a Women's Aglow meeting in Mount Pleasant. At that meeting,

Constance met JoAnn Swezey, a gracious woman. They became friends instantly, and JoAnn and her husband became Papa and Mama to Constance and me. Sister Swezey introduced us to another wonderful couple, Leon and Lynda Vernon, who lived in Grove, Oklahoma. They told us of the annual camp-meeting that they hold in the early summer at Grove Christian Center. We became part of the Vernon family. We would preach there at least once a year, and we attended the annual camp-meeting, where they had many pastors from around Oklahoma and the surrounding states. We hooked up with several of the pastors. Our weekends were becoming occupied to the point where we decided that we would start traveling full time. I gave up my job at the school cafeteria, where I had worked for three years while attending ORU. I also gave up the assistantship I had taken up as a graduate student at the Early Learning Center. We found ourselves traveling to different churches every weekend, while I continued with my graduate studies.

CHAPTER 18
GRADUATE STUDIES AT ORAL ROBERTS UNIVERSITY

After some time of prayer, I felt the Lord leading me to continue my studies at ORU. I decided to get into the graduate education program to earn an M.A. in Christian School Administration. As an international student, I was not eligible for grants and loans. ORU had given me some fair amount of scholarship money, but I still needed some money to finish paying my tuition and living expenses. It was a miracle how God always provided. Having graduated debt-free with my undergraduate degree, I had to graduate debt-free with the M.A. degree. I believed for God to provide, and He did not fail me. I finished the graduate degree debt-free.

Upon finishing the master's degree, I felt led to obtain the Doctor of Education degree. After a two-year break from school, I started the Ed.D. program in Educational Leadership in the Fall of 1998. I went to work and really worked hard. I continued to travel in ministry. Our base for ministry was expanding. In October 2002, I successfully defended my doctoral dissertation on "Vocational Education in Zimbabwe and Oklahoma." My wife and family were very encouraging of me to finish the doctoral program. I give credit to my graduate advisor, Dr. Byron McKissack, for his unwavering support and encouragement. My dissertation chair, Dr. Hallett Hullinger, was exceptional. He was very strict, but encouraging as well. I became the first black student and first international student to graduate with the Ed.D. degree from ORU in its first four-year history in 2003! I give praise to the Lord for His goodness to me.

CHAPTER 19
MISSION TO ISRAEL

In 1989, when I was a student at Christ for the Nations Institute in Dallas, I tried to go to Israel on a summer missions trip. The effort to go did not work out. In 1995, when I was a graduate student at ORU, an opportunity presented itself for me to travel to Israel with a team from CFNI. After I left Dallas, I had continued to stay in touch with one of my professors, Dr. Duane Weis. He encouraged me to join him on a mission trip to Israel. I flew down from Tulsa to Dallas to join the team. It was the middle of May, and we were going for a ten-day mission. We flew from Dallas to St. Louis, Missouri, then to Paris, France, and finally to Tel-Aviv, Israel. Upon landing in Israel, several of us got down our knees and kissed the land. It was awesome to be in the land that Jesus Christ walked. After clearing customs, we boarded a bus and headed for Jerusalem, which would be our hub while we were there.

We criss-crossed the land. We went around Jerusalem for the first couple of days. Then we traveled to Jericho on our way to Galilee. We enjoyed our time in Galilee. We were baptized in the River Jordan. We went on a boat ride across the Sea of Galilee. We enjoyed the food especially, St. Peter's fish. We went to Nazareth where Jesus was raised. We stepped into the synagogue where He went on the Sabbath. On our way back, we went to the Dead Sea, where we swam in the salty water. After we returned to Jerusalem, we went to the Garden of Gethsemane, the Upper Room, and the Garden Tomb.

One of the Saturdays, Dr. Weis asked me to preach to the team. That was one of the highlights of the mission. There were sixty-five of us on this mission. I made a connection with several of the team members. One of the people with whom I connected was Warren Mize. He is Dr. Weis' son-in-law. We became friends, and I have had the wonderful opportunity of taking my family to San Antonio, Texas, to minister in his church a number of times. I had the great opportunity to minister for Dr. Weis, after he retired from CFNI, at Grand Prairie Assembly of God. Dr. Weis preached at our annual missions banquet and convention in Tulsa.

Something happened at the end of our Israel mission that I will never forget. As we were checking in at the airport to leave Israel in Tel-Aviv, I was shocked when the airline official told me that I was not going back to America. I asked why, and he told me that I did not have a valid visa to fly to the States. I did not know that my visa had expired after my time at CFNI. Even though I had a valid student I-20 for being at ORU, my traveling visa had expired. I was taken aside by security, and they interrogated me as to why I was in Israel and what we did. I explained the whole mission. I was told that I was not able to fly back to the States until I got my visa renewed. I went to the US Embassy in Tel-Aviv several times, to try to get my visa renewed. All efforts were in vain. They advised me to go back to my home country, Zimbabwe, and to apply for the visa there. I stayed at a Lutheran Shelter while I was trying to settle my travel situation.

Friends and family started praying for me when they heard of my dilemma. Constance sought some help from friends to help with raising money for the flight from Tel-Aviv, Israel, to Harare, Zimbabwe. Pastor Frank and Elsie Adams took the lead in raising the money for me to go to Zimbabwe to renew my visa, and then to come to the States. I was in Israel for another week after the team had left. I was happy to be going home after being seven years away, but I was anxious as to whether I would get the visa. Friends and relatives were very happy to see me. I was nervous, until after I went to the US Embassy in Harare. I was so surprised at how nice they were to me. I got my visa renewed, and I picked it up the next day. The next few days, I visited with relatives before returning to the States. I was in Zimbabwe another week. Then I flew back to Tulsa, Oklahoma.

When I returned to the States, I had a great re-union with my family, church, and friends. We had been scheduled to preach in several churches. Constance was able to go to some of them which were close to Tulsa, and she did a terrific job. Immediately after my return from Israel, we started the process of applying for our green cards for permanent residence in the United States. The process took about two years before we received our green cards. Pastor Jonathan Wakefield and Harvest Church helped us get the green cards. We received our green cards in 1997.

CHAPTER 20
STEPPING OUT FOR MISSIONS

After we got our permanent residence cards, we did not have to get a visa each time we left the country. After we got our green cards, in the spring of 1997, three months later I was on my way to Africa on a month-long mission. I flew from Tulsa to Dallas and then to London. From London, I flew to Zimbabwe. I ministered in Harare for a few days, and then I flew to Nairobi, Kenya. I ministered in Kenya with our friends, Bishop Paul and Mrs. Grace Mbithi, who had just started a new church, which later grew rapidly into several ministries. From there, I flew to Uganda where a former schoolmate and pastor friend, Rev. Peter Mutebi, hosted me in Kampala. I preached my heart out for ten days. From there I went back to Nairobi, and I preached for Bishop Alois Rutivi in his 1,000-member church. Then I flew back to Harare, Zimbabwe, for final ministry, before I flew back to Tulsa. This would be the first official mission to Africa. Although the excitement of ministry had taken over, I was very happy to be back with my family.

The following year, I planned a five-week mission to five African countries with a pastor friend, Phil Platner. We left in the middle of the summer of 1998 for

Uganda. After we landed in Entebe, we were picked up by car to go to Tororo with Bishop Lokwango. We ministered in a conference there for three days. Then he took us to Soroti, where we ministered for Dr. Zerubbabel Ebangit. He was traveling overseas, but his wife hosted us wonderfully. She was a caucasian lady from Texas who had become Ugandan, of all things, in the middle of nowhere. From Soroti, we made a short stop in Mbale. Then we went to Kampala where we ministered in three churches, including the Prayer Palace. After a few days in Kampala, we flew to Nairobi, Kenya. We preached in a few churches under the leadership of Bishop Silas Owiti. In all these places, we saw God heal many and saw several saved.

From Nairobi, Kenya, we flew to Lusaka, Zambia, where we ministered for five days. We had the wonderful opportunity to speak at a ministerial fellowship in downtown Lusaka. Zambia was a little more relaxing than the other two countries that we had visited. We left for Harare, Zimbabwe, where we spent two weeks. We ministered for Rev. and Mrs. Cuthbert Makoni in their church and school. Then we traveled to Nhira Village in Murewa, a couple of hours northeast of Harare. We were in the village for a couple days, and we preached two nights as people gathered by a bonfire. As far as my parents could remember, Brother Phil was the first American ever to come to our village. From Nhira Village, we drove to Chiminya Village, about six hours away. We ministered there for a couple of days, then we drove back to Harare. Rev. and Mrs. Bartholomew Manjoro hosted us on this final leg of our visit to Harare. We ministered in their annual August conference for four days, and we had the time of our lives in ministry. This would be the conclusion of our time in Zimbabwe. After ministering for five weeks, we headed back to Oklahoma to our wives and families.

In 1999, Constance and I took our children to Zimbabwe again. We ministered and visited with family for a month. Leaving the children in Zimbabwe, Constance and I flew to Mbabane, Swaziland, and ministered there for five days with Rev. Shadreck Tsabedze in a tent crusade, where we saw many saved and healed. From Swaziland, we flew to Port Elizabeth, South Africa, where we ministered for three days with Pastor Sam Fidelis Kaseke. After that weekend's ministry, I flew back to Harare to my family.

While we were in Zimbabwe with the family, after ministry in Harare and Nhira and Chiminya Villages as well as the ministry in Swaziland and South Africa, we took a few days to go to the Victoria Falls. We traveled by public transport from Harare to Bulawayo, the second largest city in Zimbabwe, where we visited with Constance's brother, Emmanuel Chiminya, and his family for a couple of days. Then we took an overnight train to one of the seven natural wonders of the world, Victoria Falls. Our children thoroughly enjoyed walking around the waterfalls. After walking through the falls and taking pictures, we boarded a bus for the city of Hwange, where we ate dinner and preached a service for a friend, Dr. Kenneth Magwenzi. We took an overnight train back to Bulawayo. Upon arrival the next morning, we took a bus to Harare. When we arrived in Harare, we started preparing for our trip back to the United States.

God is a faithful God. We had labored in Zimbabwe, Swaziland, and South Africa for a month. We bade our friends and family good-bye to go to the Harare International Airport for our return trip back to the States. At the airport, there was a commotion that particular evening. The airline had overbooked, so they told us that we were not able to travel back to America together. Some of our family would have to go that night and others would have to go the next day. We did not want that. We wanted to travel together. They made us a deal. They gave us the option to stay that night and travel together the next day. They would reward us for the inconvenience by giving us $2,100, which we picked up in London at the British Airways customer service counter. They put us in the Sheraton Hotel for the night with dinner and breakfast. The Queen of England stayed in the Sheraton when she visited Zimbabwe. There we were, ambassadors for Christ. The next day, we went to the airport to find out that we had been booked to travel first class, and we were escorted to the first-class lounge. We traveled in first class all the way to London. The flights back to Dallas were full, and we could not find any first-class seats. Our hearts were filled with great joy for having served our Lord faithfully in Zimbabwe. The visits to Zimbabwe changed our children's lives forever. They knew what they had, which other children in Africa did not have.

In the fall of 1999, I took a three-week mission trip to East Africa with a good friend, Pastor Ron Venters, of Christ Kingdom Builders in Muskogee, Oklahoma. We flew from Tulsa to Dallas, then to London, and then to Entebe, Uganda. Our host, Pastor Moses Mbuga, welcomed us and took us to Jinja, where we preached an open-air crusade for three days. After the crusade, we preached in a few churches. While we were in Jinja, we visited the source of the Nile River. From there we went to Mbale, where we visited my friend Clement Walujo's school, and we preached in a church. We came back to Kampala and preached in a church for Pastor Venter's friend, Pastor Murefu.

After visiting Uganda, we flew to Dar-el-salam, Tanzania. Pastor Andrew Mukasa hosted us, and we preached in a few places. We saw many lives saved and healed by the power of God. From Tanzania, we flew to Nairobi, Kenya, where we were hosted by missionary friends Jim and Meg Thacker. We were in Kenya for about three days. We preached in one of the largest churches in Nairobi, All Nations Church. I preached the first morning service, and Pastor Venters preached in the second. People were saved and healed in both services. The next day, we flew back to the States with great joy that lives had been touched.

In 2000, I took a trip to East Africa again. This time I traveled with a friend and former neighbor, Jim Utpadel. Jonathan Kattam, a medical doctor from Kenya who had become a friend of both Jim and myself, introduced us to a missionary who was working in Kenya: Michael Nieswand. His ministry was rehabilitating young people who had been on the streets, and introducing them to ministry. Michael and his team came to pick us up from Jomo Kenyatta Airport upon our arrival. They drove us to Nakuru, where one of their centers was located. We were amazed to see the boys who had been washed by the blood of Jesus. They had been on the streets, but now they were singing for Jesus and seeing people come to the Lord. After a week of ministry in Nakuru, we went to Eldoret for a few days. Mostly we held open-air meetings. One particular day, we held an open-air crusade at a market. There were about 7,000 people gathered to hear the Word of God—the largest number of people that I had ever spoken to at that time. After I preached, about 2,000 of these people came forward to receive Christ as their Lord and Savior. It was such a gratifying mission. From Nairobi, we flew to Dar-el-salam, Tanzania, for a couple of days of ministry. Again Pastor Andrew Mukasa was at hand to host us for some meetings. We preached in a pastors' conference and in an open-air crusade, and we saw many saved and healed. From there, we flew back to the States. After this mission, the Lord spoke to me that in a couple of years, He was shifting my ministry to be focused in Zimbabwe. Brother Jim would return to Kenya a few more times by himself. One time he went to Kenya and joined me in Zimbabwe.

In 2001, I went to Zimbabwe with Pastor Lee Brown, who was pastor of Ratliff City Assembly of God at that time. My father, Edmond Tiripapi Nhira, had come to spend some time with us in December of 2000. So Pastor Brown, my father, and I traveled together to

Zimbabwe in June 2001. We had such a wonderful trip. My father had the comfort of traveling with people he knew, after having come by himself and being escorted everywhere. When we arrived in Harare, we were taken to the village by a rented van. We ministered in Nhira Village in Murewa for a couple of days. Several were saved and healed. We came back to the city and preached for Rev. Bartholomew Manjoro at his lunch-hour meeting and night school. We then held a two-day revival in Mabvuku. We went to Chiminya Village in Gutu, and we visited and ministered with my in-laws. Rev. and Mrs. Hasimoni Zimbeva, Constance's parents. After the village ministry, we returned to Harare to minister for Apostle Dr. Abel Sande. We stayed at his house while ministering for him, and we had a wonderful time. Pastor Brown and Rev. Sande bonded so well that he returned a couple of months later for their annual August conference with another friend. In the same summer of 2001, Constance and our son Brian went to Zimbabwe, along with Sister Lynda Vernon and her daughter Dawne, from Grove Christian Center in Oklahoma. We have assisted Sister Lynda to go to Zimbabwe three times by arranging her meetings there.

In 2002, Dr. Paul Rains, from Ellington, Missouri, and I went on a mission trip to Togo and Benin, West Africa. We met in the Atlanta Airport for the first time. All the time before, we had been talking on the phone. We flew from Atlanta to Amsterdam, Holland, and then from Amsterdam to Accra, Ghana. Brother Nadjombe Nadjombe waited for us in Accra. We spent the night in a hotel in Accra. The next day, Nadjombe drove us the long trip to Lome, Togo. From Lome, we drove to Benin, where we ministered for a few days in an open-air crusade. We planted a church in Benin, and then we went back to Togo. In Togo, we ministered in a few churches and in an open-air crusade. We also planted a church there. We had the wonderful privilege of visiting the Assembly of God Church in Basare, which was founded by the late missionaries David and Claudia Wakefield. We also saw the vocational school that they had started, and we had a burden for it to continue to grow. After criss-crossing Benin and Togo, we visited with Nadjombe and his family for a couple of days preparing for our return. Nadjombe drove us back to Accra to catch our plane back to the States. We were filled with great joy for the many lives that were changed with the gospel of Christ through our ministry. Dr. Rains has remained a wonderful friend. Our friend Nadjombe went to be with the Lord after planting over 400 churches.

In 2002, I also traveled to Kenya on a short ten-day mission. I was the guest of Bishop Mungai. We had met at Oral Roberts University, where he was in the School of Theology and Missions and I was in the Graduate School of Education. In Kenya, I taught in a leadership seminar and a women's conference. The Sunday while I was there, I preached in one of his churches in Nairobi. It was a short, but very vibrant, mission trip. After this mission, the Lord started to stir me about shifting our ministry efforts to Zimbabwe.

CHAPTER 21
ZIMBABWE MISSION

In 2002, the Lord started dealing with me about shifting our focus of ministry to establish our base of ministry in Zimbabwe. I was enjoying traveling and holding crusades in the different African countries, but God said to stop and to follow His direction. I knew the road would not be easy to start ministering in Zimbabwe because there were many large ministries and church organizations from our own home country. Our first mission to Zimbabwe was in June of 2003. We organized our first conference in the Meikles Hotel, in Harare, for four days. One hundred and sixty-two participated in that first conference. We ministered in a few churches of the pastors who attended the conference. We also visited Nhira Village in Murewa, and Chiminya Village in Gutu, and we ministered there. Rev. and Mrs. Josiah Tarukwasha hosted us in their home while we were on this mission.

The following year, 2004, we went back to Zimbabwe for our second mission. This time, Constance and I were accompanied by our boys, Jasper and Brian. We ministered in churches and in the villages. We moved the conference to the Dutch Reformed Church Hall in downtown Harare. People trickled in slowly to the conferences. This time we really needed to hear the Scripture in Zechariah 4:10, not to despise the day of small things. We had much fewer people than we expected. If we had not known that we had the Word of the Lord to hold these meetings, then we would have quit right then. We encouraged ourselves in the Lord.

Some of our friends, who were hearing about what God was doing, were interested in coming with us. In 2005, Sister Lynda Vernon and her sister Sarah, from Louisiana, joined us on the mission to Zimbabwe. This was Sister Lynda's third mission to Zimbabwe. Brother Jerry Clark came with us on this mission. This time our three children came with us as well: Jasper, Brian, and Faith. Jim Utpadel met us in Zimbabwe, coming from Kenya. Lynda and Sarah stayed at the Tarukwasha home. My sister, Marvelous Mushoshoma, had found a guest house for the rest of us by the Khopje in Harare. We were there for one night when the police came to shut the place down. They came the following morning and asked us to leave the place right away because we were operating illegally. We had to find alternative lodging that day. Our family moved to the United Baptist Center in Hatfield, Harare. We moved Brother Jerry to Pastor Ephiel Mukamuri's home. We ministered in the conferences, churches, and villages. The joy of seeing people saved and healed comforted us. Sister Lynda encouraged us time and again, as we came to the meetings, that we were not in the book of Numbers, but in the book of Acts! We started the women's conference that year. After the conferences, Rev. and

Mrs. Tarukwasha guided some of our team members to the Victoria Falls.

Jerry Clark, along with his wife Linda, would travel with us again the following year and for the next seven years. In 2006, we had the biggest group join us in Harare for the annual meetings. There were fourteen of us, including Drs. Ron and Char Meyers, missionaries who were residing in South Africa; Dr. Gwen Williams and her group of six, which included 103-year-old Rev. Ortis Clark, who passed on six years later. Each year we would add different conferences. After the conferences, we took the whole team to the Victoria Falls to tour the fascinating site. Unusually, we had aircraft trouble with the first team that we took to the Falls. The airplane had an engine problem a few minutes into the flight, and we turned back to the Falls Airport. Upon landing, one of the wheels punctured. They had to send another plane that was flying from South Africa to pick us up, and we arrived back in Harare without incident. After this, we returned to the States with great joy after having fulfilled our mission.

Pastors David and Louise Mashburn, of Living Hope Assembly in Elkins, Arkansas, joined us in 2007 for the first time to Africa. Christopher Cate, a young man from Columbia Bible College in Missouri, traveled with us that year as well. After we left, he stayed for another month to fulfill his internship hours. It became evident that the hand of God was upon Chris. He learned to expound the Scriptures in ways that he never expected. The Mashburns were such a blessing.

Our son Brian helped us host our first youth and young adults conference. Our first youth conference had a little over one hundred young people. In a few years this would grow to become the biggest conference, packing the Dutch Hall to capacity.

At this point, the nation of Zimbabwe was in great difficulty economically. The Zimbabwe dollar, which had been of equal value with the American dollar in the 1980s, had lost its value terribly. In 2008, the US dollar was equivalent to about 60,000 Zimbabwe dollars. The hyperinflation caused the country to print large bills ranging from Zim$10 to Zim$100 trillion. The country was in such economic turmoil that people were dying of hunger. The stores became empty with shop owners not able to buy inventory. We did not know how to help the situation, with so many people needing help. That year we shipped sixteen barrels of food to the people that we could get to quickly. In 2009, the nation abandoned its currency to use US dollars as the primary currency, along with the South African Rand, the British Pound, and the Botswana Pula. This stabilized the inflation. We saw the resilience of the people of Zimbabwe. Our ministry, Hope for All Nations Ministries, was as determined as ever to give the people of Zimbabwe hope in Christ Jesus. In 2008, we only had a team of four: Jerry and Linda Clark, Constance and me. The anointing was stronger than ever. The people were so happy that we came.

Between 2009 and 2013, different ones have traveled with us to Zimbabwe for missions. Some of the people who have traveled with us are: Brenda Iverson, a school teacher from Ringgold, Louisiana; Windy Clevenger, a pastor's wife from Miami, Oklahoma; Eric Parker, senior pastor of New Life International Church; Joshua Turnbull, a college student from Bristow, Oklahoma; Daniel King, a friend of Jerry Clark; Johnny Drummond, a minister and owner of a construction company from Elkins, Arkansas; Curtis Mashburn, associate and youth pastor from Elkins, Arkansas; and Philip Griffith, a businessman from Lancaster, Ohio. We have added several conferences and ministries, and they continue to grow. The conferences that we hold now are: prayer conference, leadership conference, education fellowship, business seminar, men's conference, single women's conference, couples, marriage and family conference, women in ministry conference, ladies conference, and youth and young adults conference. We hold kids crusades throughout the city of Harare, and we minister in schools. We also hold revivals in churches and we minister in villages.

I attribute the success of our ministry in Zimbabwe and the United States to God's answer to prayer, as well as to the relationships that God has given us. From the beginnings of our ministry, we formed two ministry boards: one in the States, and another in Zimbabwe. God has given us servant leaders who are great advisors. Proverbs 11:14 says, "Where there is no counsel, the people fall; but in the multitude of counselors there is safety." At each end, we have an advisory board and a board of directors. The USA board is comprised of several advisory board members and a seven-member board of directors. The Zimbabwe board is comprised of many advisory board members and a twelve-member board of directors. All these are mature evangelical men and women from different church backgrounds. Some of them are heads of their denominations. Our ministry is about fostering the unity of the body of Christ, and not about dividing it. Before leaving for heaven, Jesus gave a command to the church: "A new commandment I give to you, that you love one another; as I have loved you, that you also love one another. By this all will know that you are My disciples, if you have love for one another" (John 13:34-35). He prayed "that they all may be one, as You, Father, are in Me, and I in You; that they also may be one in Us, that the world may believe that you sent Me" (John 17:21). We are thankful to God for our teams, both in the United States and in Zimbabwe, and all those who support our ministry, for what they offer to the body of Christ.

CHAPTER 22
FURTHERING EDUCATION AT UNIVERSITY OF PHEONIX, LIBERTY UNIVERSITY, AND NORTHCENTRAL UNIVERSITY

After I graduated from Oral Roberts University in 2003 with my third degree, friends and family started asking me what I was going to do. I told them that the Lord had called me to preach the gospel, and that I was continuing to preach. I took a two-year break from school and continued to preach. In the fall of 2005, I decided to further my education. Someone told me about an online school, University of Phoenix, that had a campus in Tulsa. Their main campus was in Phoenix, Arizona, but they also had many campuses around the United States. I checked it out: they had a "flex net" program which combined going to campus the first day of school for the whole day, and then six weeks of working online with a teacher and a cohort. Then students would come to campus again on the last day of school for the whole day. I enrolled in the MBA program in general business. I worked hard, and in two years I finished the program and went to graduate in Oklahoma City in July 2007. I met wonderful instructors and students who encouraged me to be involved in business as a minister. I always felt the Lord wanted me to know how to run a business since He was preparing us for a big ministry.

I took a one-semester break after graduating from University of Phoenix. While on this break, the Lord began to deal with me about enrolling in a theology program. I had gained training in education and business, and now I felt the need to train in the Word of God. I came across a completely online program at Liberty Baptist Theological Seminary at Liberty University in Lynchburg, Virginia. I enrolled in the Master of Divinity (MDiv) program in Evangelism and Church Growth, and I started in the spring of 2008. Only nine credit hours from my previous program at ORU transferred to the LU program. Therefore, I had 81 credit hours to complete. I went to work, and in three years I finished the MDiv program and graduated in 2011. I met many friends online who would be a great blessing and encouragement to our ministry.

Towards the end of the MDiv program, I enrolled in the Doctor of Ministry program at Liberty Baptist Seminary. I felt confirmation for me to proceed to the DMin program. This program would only allow me to do one class online, which I was accustomed to doing. For the other 21 credit hours, I would have to go to the campus seven times, and nine credits would be from the dissertation part, which I would work on from home. I was determined to do it! I went to Liberty University campus seven times, and I worked hard. I finished the course work in two years. Then I went on to work on the dissertation project.

One of the times, I stayed in the Wingate Hotel on the fourth floor in a room overlooking the Liberty University campus. I was challenged, and I kept looking around the campus each day that I was there for six days. The Holy Spirit challenged me to one day build a university like this for our people in Zimbabwe. The challenge was reiterated as the one which I had received when I got to the Oral Roberts University. I really thank God for the opportunities that He gave me to prepare myself for the ministry and work that He had ahead for me and my wife.

Upon the completion of the DMin degree at Liberty University, the Lord opened another door, which I believe is the final phase of my educational journey and preparation for what God has for me to accomplish in expanding the Great Commission. I enrolled at Northcentral University, in Prescott, Arizona, in the fall of 2014, to pursue a PhD in Global Training and Development. This education is beneficial as we minister in the calling that we have received from the Lord.

CHAPTER 23
EXPANDING THE AMERICAN MISSION

My family and I have had the wonderful opportunity of preaching in over 400 churches in eighteen states in the United States. Pastors of churches will always have us many times after we visit and preach one time. The message that God gave us encourages the church to rise up and to be the church that God intended. Our children learned to minister for the Lord from young ages. They started singing in our meetings. They sang well-known children's songs, and then they started singing from soundtracks. Our son, Brian, took music to the next level. He was tutored by his high school teachers. When he enrolled in Oral Roberts University, they spotted his singing talents and he was chosen to be a member of the praise and worship team for the chapel services. Brian has recorded sixteen songs that are on CD. These can be obtained through his website: www.briannhira.com. He has sung for the Detroit Tigers baseball, Tulsa Drillers baseball, Oklahoma City Thunder NBA, Tulsa Shock WNBA, OU basketball, Cancer Treatment Centers of America annual banquet, and at the inauguration of the Oral Roberts University fourth president, Dr. Billy Wilson. Our other children love God and continue to serve God in churches.

In 2004, we began holding mission banquets for our missions ministry. These have been a big source of financial support to change nations. These banquets have been growing steadily, and they promise to grow bigger. These meetings bring together friends, partners, and pro-visionaries. At these meetings, our team reports what Hope for All Nations Ministries is doing locally and in Zimbabwe. Previous mission team members get to share their experiences from overseas. The audience is given the opportunity to participate in our missions ministry in Zimbabwe, Africa.

CHAPTER 24
RAISING CHAMPION CHILDREN

For Constance and me, one of the joys of our lives has been raising our four children. We always thank God for giving us wonderful children. Ten months after we got married the Lord blessed us with a beautiful girl. We named her Prosper. She was born at Harare Hospital in Zimbabwe in 1983. As our native custom is, Constance had to leave our home to go back to her parents to deliver the first baby among her parents and relatives. Because her parents were in the village, she had to go stay with her brother, Flavian, who lived in Westwood, Harare. Her mother came to the city to be with her during those last days before delivery. At that time, we had been staying at the Bible school in Glen Norah, where I was administering the reading and writing program for the school. It was so thrilling for me to go to my brother-in-law's house to see and hold my first baby for the first time. After a few days, they brought the baby to our place at the Bible school. She was such a joy to have. She made our quiet home lively.

While we were pastoring at Tafara in Harare, we were blessed with another child, a boy this time. He was born at Harare Hospital in Zimbabwe in 1985. We named him Jasper. This time Constance did not have to go to her parents or relatives to deliver the baby. She went to the nearby clinic from our house. The clinic transported her to the main hospital. After Jasper was delivered, I had the wonderful opportunity to go to the hospital to see my baby boy. The next day I came back to the hospital and we took him to the parsonage. Now we had two children! There was more activity in the home. We dedicated our children to the Lord a few months after each one was born.

Four years after Jasper was born, I moved to the United States for further studies. Constance followed a year later with Prosper and Jasper. What a reunion it was to see them at the Dallas-Fort Worth Airport! About two years later the Lord blessed us with another boy. He was born in 1992 at the Doctors' Hospital in Tulsa, Oklahoma. We named him Brian, which means "strong". One lady with whom we were acquainted came to the hospital, and she prophesied over him and said that he would be mightily used by God. She said that we should call his name "John". That became his middle name. When Brian was born, I had the glorious experience of going to the hospital to be beside my wife during labor. It was indeed a touching experience. I encouraged Constance throughout the twelve hours of labor. Now we had three children, and at the same time, I had to go to university full-time and work for this crew to live.

Our last child came in 1995 at Hillcrest Medical Center in Tulsa. We named her Faith. She became a joy to the family. Again, I had the privilege of being with Constance when she was delivered. As our children were growing up, Constance stayed home with them as she did not have a permit to work outside the home then. She imparted her motherliness into them.

As our children were growing up, the Lord revealed to us to read the Bible with them night after night. We would each take turns reading a chapter from the Word of God before going to bed. We were able to read through the Bible six times with our children before they started working and going to college. We did not do a Bible study, we just read with them. Each night we would pray with them before retiring to bed. Each one would have a day of the week when he or she led the family in prayer. One other thing that bound us together as a family has been traveling together for ministry. From 1993 until 2011, the children traveled with us, each then leaving the ministry as he or she started working. We enjoyed them traveling with us, and hopefully they enjoyed it as well. From how they all have turned out, they appreciated their upbringing. They were in a church or two each Sunday, to where it became a custom for them to be in church. They started singing in different churches from a young age, and all became wonderful singers. Brian, from the ministry and school, took his singing to another level and has become a wonderful recording artist.

We never allowed our children to miss a day of school for no apparent reason. We are proud of how each one of our children has turned out. Prosper, our oldest child, is a voracious reader. She married a wonderful young man, Gary from Louisiana, and has blessed us with two wonderful grandbabies: Nhira Lu Iverson and Tre Gary Iverson III. Jasper skipped grade 12 because he had been held back in the first grade. After grade 11, he took the GED and desired to get ahead, so he advanced to college. He went to Tulsa Community College and then proceeded to Oklahoma State University, where he graduated with a Bachelor of Science degree in business. He then went on to graduate school at Oral Roberts University, and he earned a Master of Management degree. He has held a managerial position with a car rental company in Tulsa, Oklahoma. He is now a consultant and helps many young people advance with their lives.

Two weeks into his first semester at Oral Roberts University, Brian was selected to sing on the ORU praise team as a worship leader. He traveled with the team and the president, singing in major events in several cities. During his time in college, Brian wrote and recorded sixteen songs, which elevated him to a young celebrity in Oklahoma. Brian graduated with honors with a Bachelor of Science degree in Interpersonal and Organizational Communication. He was the student response speaker for the ORU graduating class of 2014. He has travelled to Africa with us on numerous occasions. Upon graduation, he joined the staff of one of the largest churches in Tulsa as a music minister. Pastor Ron Woods did not waste time—he immediately asked Brian to be one of his praise and worship leaders at The Assembly in Broken Arrow, Oklahoma. Brian honored us tremendously when he participated as a contestant in Season 10 of

"The Voice"! After Brian sang "Happy," the judges asked him to sing "Jesus Loves Me" (which he started singing at an early age when traveling with us in churches), and he received a standing ovation from the judges and the crowd on NBC.

As I drove Faith to school when she was in intermediate school, each morning I asked her to recite, "I feel good. I feel great. I feel terrific!" And she added, "I feel rich!" When Faith was a freshman at Jenks High School, they tested the class for reading, and her reading level was college level. We attribute that to her reading the Bible with us in our home. While a junior in high school, Faith took concurrent college classes at Tulsa Community College, and she graduated a semester early from high school. Every one of our immediate family members had gone to Oral Roberts University, but Faith said, "I am not going to be a Golden Eagle, I am going to be a Sooner." So she went to Oklahoma University, where she started as a sophomore because of the courses she had taken at TCC. She became one of the praise and worship leaders at Truth Church in Norman, Oklahoma. As every one of our children did, she was responsible for her college finances. Paying for their college has taught our children to be responsible people. Constance and I are proud parents of these four champions for Christ. As they have been growing, we consistently pray for their future spouses. We believe with them for the right mates.

CHAPTER 25
CELEBRATING 25 YEARS OF MARRIAGE

On May 1, 2007, Constance and I were married 25 years, and both of us turned 50 years of age in 2007! We had a ceremony renewing our vows to celebrate our silver anniversary at Chapel in the Woods, Harvest Church, in Tulsa, Oklahoma. Pastor Jonathan Wakefield officiated the ceremony. There was cause to celebrate! We were celebrating the journey of 25 years together. We never fought physically in those twenty-five years. We only once in a while had moments of intense fellowship. Our journey has been exciting. To celebrate this milestone, we planned to go on a cruise. We came back from our annual mission to Zimbabwe in June of 2007, excited to go on our first-ever cruise. We flew from Tulsa to Seattle, Washington. We spent a night in a motel, then we boarded the ship the next day. We set sail that afternoon for the 7-day cruise. We were part of the Focus on the Family cruise group. There were about 900 attending this conference on the ship. Of course there were several others doing their own things. We attended the conference in the morning, and in the afternoon we just relaxed as we wished in our rooms or we walked around the ship enjoying the view as it cruised. There was so much food—different kinds of food.

After a couple of days, we landed at the town of Juneau, Alaska. We went off the ship to get a little sunshine. Unfortunately it was raining in Alaska, but we cherished the opportunity to get out and walk on land. We went window shopping, and we bought swimming suits to swim on the ship. After a while, we began the return journey. This time we sailed to Vancouver, Canada, then onward back to Seattle. It was a gratifying trip. On this cruise, we met long-lasting friends, Philip and Janet Griffith. Phil traveled to Zimbabwe for our annual mission in 2009, and several more times after that first trip. They have been such blessings. It was indeed a cruise to remember. We will cherish every memory of it.

We have always remembered our anniversary day by taking a day off from our weekly routines. When Constance and I first got married, we went on our first anniversary outing by going to a motel owned and operated by a church in Harare. We went to the Trade Fair in Bulawayo one time. On another anniversary, we spent a weekend in one of our elders' homes who lived in the countryside. Sometimes we would go for breakfast, lunch, or dinner. To go on a weeklong cruise was tremendous for us. During the ceremony where we repeated our vows, I told Constance, in front of friends and family, "If you stick with me, I will take you to places you never dreamed of." An Alaskan cruise was one of them. No success can compensate for failure in the home; therefore, we have endeavored to live well together, and to raise champion and godly children. Our children always attest that they have seen an exemplary marriage.

CHAPTER 26
GUIDING PRINCIPLES

There are six principles that have guided my life along with my family: the fear of the Lord, giving, praying, fasting, the Word of God, and the Holy Spirit. These principles are enumerated in Acts 10 of the Scriptures. I believe them with all my heart, and I have seen God blessing my family and me. From the time when I gave my life to Christ in September 1978, I decided to fear God all my life. I am not afraid of God, but I give Him reverence. That is the fear that I am talking about. This is the kind of fear that God is looking for from His creation.

After I gave my life to Christ, I started attending a church that believed and practiced these principles that I am talking about. The church taught us to give to God. They taught us to give of our time, talents, and treasures. I never missed church service for anything. When there was a work day or activities at church, I made time to be there. I still have a passion for the Lord's house. There are very few occasions when I miss church service. Even when it snows where I am, I will "crawl" to any open church nearby. As a youth at my church, I sang in the church choir and in the young men's choir, I participated in a prayer band, a revival band, Sunday school, and youth program. I started giving my tithes to God soon after I got saved. I developed a passion to give, even in small ways.

When I gave my life to Christ at the age of 21, I was privileged to be a member of a church that prayed a lot. Monday was fasting and prayer day. We fasted the whole day, and we came to church in the evening for corporate prayer. Friday was overnight prayer day at the church. Sometimes the leadership of the church would schedule a whole week of fasting and praying at the church. I developed a personal early-morning prayer discipline. I would wake up early in the morning to pray for an hour before heading to work. I also started a prayer group of young men from the church. Once a month, we would go up the hills of the nearby suburb of Warren Park in Harare for overnight prayer. When I started pastoring, I would rise early to pray, and I spent many Saturdays in prayer at the church in preparation for the services on Sunday. My prayer life was greatly enhanced when I went to Christ for the Nations Institute for further studies. It was a school of prayer. I instituted prayer in my family. Constance and I started our marriage at a Bible school in prayer. For a whole year we went to the school chapel early in the morning for prayer, even when she was pregnant with our first child. We have taught our children to pray. As they were growing up, each family member had a day of leading prayer. This has bound us together as a family. We have learned not only that prayer works, but that prayer *is* work. It takes desire and discipline to pray. When we desire and discipline ourselves to pray, prayer becomes a delight. The people who pray together, stay together. God does nothing except in answer to prayer. One can only go as far as prayer will take him or her.

Another principle that I have lived by is fasting. Some of the challenges that we face in life are only moved by prayer and fasting. In Matthew 17:21, Jesus said, "This kind does not go away except by prayer and fasting." For twenty years I fasted for three days and three nights once a month. All the men and women that God used in Bible days were men and women of prayer and fasting. Moses received the law on Mt. Sinai after fasting for forty days. David became the greatest king that Israel had because he fasted and prayed. Esther delivered the children of Israel from the hand of Haman by calling a three-day time of prayer and fasting. Daniel, Shadrach, Meshach, and Abednego rose to a place of prominence in Babylon because they knew how to pray and fast. The Apostle Paul established a string of vibrant churches in Asia Minor because he prayed and fasted. Jesus Christ started His ministry with prayer and fasting. Prayer without fasting is weak. Fasting without prayer is only dieting. I have learned to intermingle my prayer life with fasting. This makes a big difference.

Fifteen times I have read the Bible through. Six of these I read with my wife and children. If you do not put the Word in your children, someone will put something else in them. Constance and I decided to put God's Word in our children, and we are happy that we did. The Word of God is powerful. It changes lives. It cleans lives. The Scriptures say that "In the beginning was the Word, and the Word was with God, and the Word was God. . . . And the Word became flesh and dwelt among us" (John 1:1, 14). It dwelt among us as Christ. When we take His Word into us, then we become like Him. Want to become like Christ? Read His Word! Hear the Word!

Acts 10:44 says, "While Peter was still speaking these words, the Holy Spirit fell upon all those who heard the word." When I gave my life to Christ, I became very hungry for His Word. I would wake up in the middle of the night to read the Bible. Soon after this, I received the Holy Spirit in a church service at Mufakose, in Harare. The prophet said, "Not by might nor by power, but by My Spirit says the Lord of hosts (Zechariah 4:6). The Holy Spirit has played an important part since I gave my life to Christ. I am where I am because of the leading of the Holy Spirit.

Cornelius used these principles. I followed these principles, and I am still following them. Methods may change, but principles never change. When we follow these biblical principles, we will live the kind of life that God intended for us to live.

CHAPTER 27
VISION

While I was in Bible school in Harare, Zimbabwe, the Lord showed me the vision that I was to follow. My vision was to travel to many countries, to bring many into the kingdom of God, and to disciple many for the end-time harvest. This was confirmation of what I had already started doing. I had joined a youth group at the church to go to sing and to preach the gospel under the streetlights. I developed a passion for seeking God in my lodging room. For 20 years, I set aside three days and three nights for total fasting, from 1980 to 2000. In 1981, in a vision, I saw the young lady whom I was going to marry while I was in the middle of a time of prayer and fasting. Ten days after we got married, Constance and I obeyed God and went to Bible school.

The Lord helped us raise a God-fearing family. He blessed us with two wonderful girls and two great boys. They are champions for Christ. The Lord has given each of them visions to serve the Lord. Constance and I had the wonderful opportunity of pastoring three wonderful churches at the beginning of our marriage. At two of the churches, we had to go and troubleshoot some problems that had been going on at those churches. Each of the three churches that we pastored doubled in size within the duration of our tenures there, each lasting a year to two years. We took the churches from within the four walls out to where the people were. We ministered to people where they lived and worked. The church was a training ground for believers. Their mission field was in their homes and neighborhoods and where they worked. We developed leaders out of many of those who were willing to serve God in different leadership positions.

In preparation for fulfilling the vision of bringing millions into the kingdom of God, the Lord opened doors of opportunity to prepare for this great mandate. The great leaders of old were great leaders because they were great learners. In the Bible, Moses became one of the greatest leaders of all time because he was a learner. He received a great education at the palace of Pharaoh. Solomon produced great wisdom because he had received the greatest education at King David's palace. Wisdom is the application of knowledge. The Apostle Paul wrote about two-thirds of the New Testament because he was a great learner before God called him to the ministry. Some say that he was well-educated, that he had the equivalent of three doctoral degrees.

When the Lord opened the door to come to America, I decided I was not going to waste time. In twenty-six years, I worked on seven degrees. All of them were directly or indirectly related to ministry. Whatever I do, I like to see growth. We have watched and seen the growth of Hope for All Nations Ministries—the ministry that Constance and I started—and we are yet to see where God will take it.

In my early years of schooling in the United States, the Lord gave me a vision to start a university in my home country of Zimbabwe. He put in me the burning desire to build a university that will train men and women for vocations and ministry. My first doctoral dissertation was entitled, "Vocational Technical Education in Zimbabwe and Oklahoma." I compared the two programs in an attempt to see what can be done in Zimbabwe from the Oklahoma model, which was one of the best programs in America. My second doctoral thesis project was on "Short-Term Missions: Zimbabwe Missions as a Model for Africa." I believe that this project is a model for reaching the world, not just Africa. We want to build a university of stature that will change many people's lives for generations to come, as the Lord tarries. We will start with building a high school, and then proceed to the construction of the university.

CHAPTER 28
HOPE CENTER ZIMBABWE

We started Hope for All Nations Ministries International with no budget and no board. We just had the burning desire to bring churches and ministries together. The theme of Hope for All Nations has been, and still is, "Connecting the body of Christ together to fulfill the Great Commission and live the abundant life of Christ." Our first conference was at the Meikles Hotel in Harare. It was attended by people from different denominations and church backgrounds. The following year, we moved the conferences to the Dutch Reformed Church auditorium in downtown Harare, which became the home of Hope for All Nations Ministries for 11 years.

We tried to look for offices in and around Harare, but nothing worked out. The Lord gave us the idea of buying land to construct our own buildings. About a year or so later, we started constructing our own buildings in phases. Phase 1 was buying the land, phase 2 was building the cabin where the caretaker would stay, phase 3 would be the construction of the office cottage, and phase 4 would be construction of the main building. The main building would house multi-purpose rooms for offices and guest bedrooms, for the purpose of training local leaders and housing mission teams for evangelism. This is going to be the headquarters of Hope for All Nations Ministries International. We are believing for the university campus to be located at a different place in Zimbabwe. There we will build multi-purpose buildings. It will be a center for learning and world evangelism. A great conference center will be built there at the university and center for world evangelism.

CHAPTER 29
SUMMARY

Looking back at this journey, it has not been an easy road, but it has been a worthwhile ride. I thank the Lord for putting me on this planet for such a time as this. A little while ago, I had the privilege to go back to the village where I grew up. Some of the trees on the plantation that my father raised many years ago are still there. The houses are no longer there. My parents moved to another village two-hours' drive away in Mangwende, Murewa. They built new houses. The people who now occupy the place where we used to live also built new houses. It was a touching moment to revisit the place where this journey all began. It was interesting to visit the place where I attended high school, and to present a gift of appreciation for the school library.

As I look back, I thank the Lord for what He has done in my life. I did not grow up in an affluent family. We were raised on subsistence farming. We were not strong believers in the Lord, either. The few times that I went to the village church, and the opportunity I had to go to Murewa United Methodist High School, prepared my life for what I am now. My first job as a school teacher in the rural areas prepared me for life in the world. I always think of my cousin Bernard Nhira, who hosted me in his home for seven months when I first went to live in the city of Harare. I got a job in the city at Textbook Sales Book Center, and I was born again at a church while I was staying in his home. My sister Charity introduced me to Christ, whom I now love and serve with all my heart. I met the love of my life, Constance, at a church in Kambuzuma, when I was working at the Standard Chartered Bank. Ten days after our wedding, we moved to Africa Multi-Nation for Christ Institute for ministry training. She has stood with me since we got married, and I promised to take her to places she never dreamed of. Pastoring in Zimbabwe for six years prepared us for an effective traveling ministry in the United States.

My time at Christ for the Nations in Dallas, Texas, was so special for me: I prayed like I had never done before. That opened the great door to go to Oral Roberts University in Tulsa, Oklahoma, and for my family to follow. There is power in plugging into a local church, regardless of its size. To be successful in life and ministry, it is important to be accountable to some people who can speak into your life. Leading the African Christian Fellowship Tulsa Chapter summoned my leadership capabilities and launched me into the traveling ministry, from which we have preached in over 400 churches in eighteen states. I cannot express in words how thankful I am to God for the great opportunity that He afforded me to go to some of the finest universities in America: Oral Roberts University,

University of Phoenix, Liberty University, and Northcentral University.

My launch into missions was in Jerusalem, Israel, in 1995. During this mission, Dr. Duane Weis offered me the opportunity to preach to the mission team in a hotel in Jerusalem. Since that time, I have traveled on numerous occasions to several countries for crusades, conferences, revivals, and for ministry in schools and villages.

I thank God for the four wonderful children with whom God blessed us. God gave us champion children who are all chasing their dreams as they serve the Lord. We brought them up in the nurture and admonition of the Lord. Six times we read through the Bible with our children in our home, reading three to five chapters a day. I thank God for a great son-in-law and the wonderful grandchildren that we have, and we are itching for more. Six principles are guiding our family: the fear of the Lord, giving, praying, fasting, the Word of God, and the Holy Spirit.

CHAPTER 30
EPILOGUE

The stage is set. I believe that Constance and I are a miracle ready to explode and do the greater works that God created us to do. The harvest is ripe and ready. With your prayers and support, together we are going to change our generation. Souls are waiting to hear the gospel. We are ready to go into every person's world. From the Hope Center, leaders are going to be launched all over the world to witness and to preach the gospel of Jesus Christ.

Our vision is to bring millions into the kingdom of God. We are called to evangelize, disciple, and educate many, using all available means. Already we have ushered many who have come into the kingdom. We have helped and encouraged many to start vibrant Christian schools. Evangelism is our supreme task, and discipleship is our strategy. Let us work together while it is still day. One day we will rest from our labors, and our works will follow us. Let us invest our lives, talents, and substance into the kingdom of God.

C. S. Lewis said, "There are no ordinary people. You have never talked to a mere mortal." We are special in the eyes of God. We are created in the image of God

(Genesis 1:27). The Scriptures say, "I will praise You, for I am fearfully and wonderfully made; marvelous are Your works" (Psalm 139:14). God knew us before we were born. He also says, "I know the plans I have for you, plans for good and not evil, to give you a future and a hope"(Jeremiah 29:11).

God loves each one of us so much that He "gave us His only Son, that whoever believes in him shall not perish, but have everlasting life" (John 3:16). "He who believes and is baptized will be saved; but he who does not believe will be condemned" (Mark 16:15). "Believers will lay hands on the sick and they will recover" (Mark 16:18). "The people who know their God shall be strong and do great exploits" (Daniel 11:32). "Greater works shall you do" (John 14:12).

Jesus Christ said, "But you shall receive power when the Holy Spirit has come upon you; and you shall be witnesses to Me in Jerusalem, and in all Judea and Samaria, and to the end of the earth" (Acts 1:8). Because you believed the Lord, be inspired to do more for God. Rise up and go to the next level of your service to God. Invest in the kingdom of God.

If you have not trusted in Jesus Christ for your salvation, please do so today. Pray this prayer from the bottom of your heart:

Lord Jesus Christ, thank you for coming to die for me on the cross. Thank you for dying and rising again so that my sins would be forgiven, so that I could live with you forever. Right now I ask you to be my Lord and Savior. From today, I choose to follow you all the days of my life. Come into my heart right now and be Lord of my life. I will read the Bible and pray every day. I will find a church near me to be plugged in, so I can grow in knowing you and in fellowshipping with other believers. I choose to follow you and serve you all the days of my life. Thank you, Lord Jesus, for forgiving me and for writing my name in your book of life. Amen.

If you prayed this prayer, I believe that you are born again. Do not draw back. Together we are going to change our generation for the glory of God.

AFTERWORD

I have known Dr. Edwell Nhira since 1993. He and his wife Constance joined Harvest Church here in Tulsa along with their family at that time. I soon discovered that he was a man of prayer with the call of God on his life. For many years we have prayed together in weekly prayer meetings at the church. He is a dedicated missionary evangelist with a passion for people to be saved and strengthened in their faith. He has traveled extensively to hundreds of churches in the United States and many African countries.

Dr. Nhira earned a Bachelors degree, three Masters degrees, and studied for three Doctorates. He is very diligent in life and ministry. He and his wife conduct crusades, conferences, revival meetings, and training seminars annually in Zimbabwe, Africa.

This book is the story of his journey from a small village in Zimbabwe to significant academic achievement and extensive ministry experience in the United States and Africa. Having grown up myself in West Africa, I can say that he made unusual progress in academics and ministry. His goals for the future outlined in this book are impressive. He gives God all the glory for everything He has done through him.

Rev. Jonathan Wakefield, DMin.
Senior Pastor
Harvest Church
Tulsa, Oklahoma

ABOUT THE AUTHOR

Edwell Nhira is a native of Murewa, Zimbabwe, Africa. He is a missionary evangelist, conference speaker, businessman, and educator. Dr. Nhira is founder of Hope For All Nations Ministries International, with offices in Tulsa, Oklahoma, and Harare, Zimbabwe.

Edwell Nhira earned a BA in Evangelism, an MA in Education, and an EdD in Educational Leadership from Oral Roberts University in Tulsa, Oklahoma. He also earned an MBA from University of Phoenix. He earned an MDiv in Evangelism and Church Growth and a DMin from Liberty University in Lynchburg, Virginia. He studied for his PhD in Global Training Development at Northcentral University in Arizona. He is listed in Who's Who in American Universities and Colleges. He graduated from Christ for the Nations Institute in Dallas, Texas, and Africa Multi-Nation for Christ Institute in Harare, Zimbabwe. Edwell Nhira attended the Billy Graham School of Evangelism in Minneapolis, Minnesota, and Denver, Colorado. He has preached in the Caribbean, Israel, and several African countries. He and his wife have preached in about 500 churches in Oklahoma and the surrounding states.

Edwell and his wife, Constance Nhira, have been married since 1982. They pastored in Zimbabwe for six years before moving to the United States. They have four children: Prosper, Jasper, Brian, and Faith. Their daughter, Prosper, married Gary Iverson II from Louisiana, and they gave the Nhiras two wonderful grandchildren, Nhira Lu Iverson and Tre Gary Iverson III, by the time of writing of this book.

Dr. Nhira has a vision to travel the continent of Africa and the world preaching the gospel of Jesus Christ, and to establish a Christian university in Zimbabwe to train men and women for vocations, technology, and ministry. He once worked as a school teacher in Maramba and Murewa, in Zimbabwe. He also worked as an accounts clerk at Textbook Sales Book Center, and as a bank clerk at Standard Chartered Bank. He entered the Christian ministry in 1982, before moving to the United States in December 1988 for further studies. While he was pastoring, he was also the administrator of a secondary school in Harare, Zimbabwe, and helped establish several dressmaking and cookery schools.

Edwell Nhira has a heart for souls to come to God through believing in Jesus Christ, and to disciple and educate many. He has a vision to bring millions into the kingdom, and to educate and train many from all over Africa and the world for the work of God.

Contact information:
Edwell Nhira
P. O. Box 722, Jenks, OK 74037, USA
Tel: 918.808.8189
Email: drnhira@sbcglobal.net
Web site: www.hopeforallnations.com
Or
Edwell Nhira
C/O No. 7 Ruskin Lane
Strathavan, Harare
Zimbabwe
Tel: 011-263-4-303728

Called to change a generation

Attending daughter Prosper's wedding in Louisiana

Itinerating with the family preaching the gospel

A visit to Rukariro School (my former primary school) 45 years later

The growing Edwell and Constance Nhira family

Made in the USA
Middletown, DE
25 September 2019